West Col Alpine Guides

CENTRAL SWITZERLAND

Series code A10

West Col Alpine Guides

Bregaglia West
Bernina Alps
Maritime Alps
Graians West
Graians East
Dents du Midi
Engelhörner & Salbitschijen
Central Switzerland
Ortler Alps
Otztal Alps

in preparation
Kaisergebirge
Karwendel
Wetterstein
North-East Switzerland

Alpine Club Guides

Mont Blanc Range Vol. I
Mont Blanc Range Vol. II
Pennine Alps Vol. I
Pennine Alps Vol. II
Dolomites Vol. I
Dolomites Vol. II
Dauphiné Alps & Vercors
Bernese Alps

WEST COL ALPINE GUIDES

Central Switzerland
GRIMSEL · FURKA · SUSTEN

a guide for walkers and climbers

JEREMY O. TALBOT

West Col Productions

First published in Great Britain 1969 by
West Col Productions
1 Meadow Close, Goring, Reading, RG8 0AP

Copyright © 1969 by J. O. Talbot

SBN   901516   05   8

The metric system and international
standards and symbols are used in this guidebook

Publisher: Pamela S. Collomb
Managing Editor: Robin G. Collomb
General Editors: Jeremy O. Talbot
                Walt Unsworth

 International grading system

Text set in Monotype Grotesque 215 and 216
Printed in England by Bradley & Son Ltd, Crown Press,
Caxton Street, Reading

CONTENTS

ILLUSTRATIONS

ABBREVIATIONS

approx.	approximately
c.	circa. (approx.)
E	East
Gr.	Gross
h.	hour(s)
Kl.	Klein
L	left
LK.	Swiss map
m.	metres
min.	minute(s)
mtn.	mountain
N	North
Ob.	Ober
pt.	point
R	right
S	South
SAC	Swiss Alpine Club
var.	variation
W	West

NB. Other directions appearing in the guidebook, e.g. SW, NE (south-west, north-east), etc., will be taken as read.

Note on diagrams

It has not been possible to represent every route described in the guidebook. On the whole routes not shown in diagrams can be traced without difficulty from details given in the descriptions and in conjunction with the recommended maps.

In diagrams dashes indicate visible portion of routes, dotted lines concealed parts, or ridge outlines. Page numbers of relevant diagrams are given at the end of the introduction of each climb.

INTRODUCTION

As defined for this guidebook Central Switzerland is an area of
wild outstanding beauty lying E of the main Oberland range.
So far it is unspoilt by modern development, which has marred
other mtn. groups in the Alps. Despite the notable absence of
cable lifts, all parts of the area are within easy access from one
of three road passes; the Grimsel, Furka and Susten; this
famous trinity encompasses the entire region.

The guide is not selected and the region has been dealt with
comprehensively in an attempt to meet the requirements of all
who wish to visit the area. All routes of interest in all degrees
of difficulty have been included and only a few second rate
ones are omitted.

Mountain exploration in the area has followed much the same
pattern as throughout the rest of the Alps. The main peaks and
most important passes were climbed in the 19th century,
followed by a steady progression to the 1930s. During this
latter period, as elsewhere, there was an upsurge of interest in
finding more difficult routes. Many of the climbs produced in
this era, especially those done by Guido Massetto and the
brothers Alfred and Otto Amstad, are still good classics and
till the 1950s were ranked among the hardest. After this date
constant activity on steeper walls and facets has and is still
yielding an impressive list of VI° routes, on mtns. such as the
Büelenhorn, Dammazwillinge and Bergseeschijen. These
were once relatively insignificant and unknown and have
suddenly come to the forefront of popularity. Naturally this
development has been the preserve of Swiss climbers, such as
Max Niedermann, K. Grüter, F. Anderrüti, Sepp Inwyler, Moses
Gamma and many others.

The author has spent several seasons in the area, doing most
of the walks, classic routes and a number of extreme climbs.
When it has not been possible to acquire personal knowledge,
several local experts have been consulted for their views and
opinions.

10

It must be emphasised that some routes cannot always be guaranteed 100 per cent accurate in description or location. The popularity of the mtns. is relatively new and it will take several years before the degree of accuracy accepted and known in other more familiar ranges is attained. Original notes on climbs often become quickly out-dated with new and better variations, access and descents vary until the best is finally accepted. The necessity for mountaineering skill in route finding both on and off the mtn. adds a certain charm which is often lacking on many well-trodden peaks round the more familiar resorts.

Topography

This is a highly compact mtn. group yet it follows a relatively simple and uncomplicated pattern. The range consists of huge ridges running S to N; the only exception is the Gletschhorn–Müeterlishorn ridge which follows a line W to E. The central massif is heavily glaciated; the largest system is the Trift, Damma and Rhone glaciers. Geologically the mtns. are composed of Aare granite which must be ranked with the hardest and finest rock in the Alps, affording splendid climbing on a par with the Bregaglia and Mont Blanc ranges.

The district is perfectly isolated from surrounding mtn. ranges by four main valley systems. To the E the Haslital, NW the Gadmental, NE the Meiental and lastly the Urseren to the SE. The Grimsel, Susten and Furka passes follow these valleys respectively. A characteristic of this area is the marked contrast between each; the savage rocky scenery of the Grimsel; the featureless trough of the Urseren and the beautiful fertile Gadmental – the typical idyllic Swiss scene.

Weather

A difficult subject on which to make any definite remarks. Generally the weather is a little better than the main Bernese Alps, but not much. The main advantage is that many climbs, especially on the rock peaks, are quite low in altitude and consequently clear quite quickly.

Approaches and Transport services

From Britain there are frequent daily express trains and air flights to Basel. From here it is best to take a train to Lucerne, via Olten, and then a train to Interlaken over the Brunig pass, alighting at Meiringen. The postal bus service leaves from the station at fairly frequent intervals for all three passes (Grimsel, Furka or Susten). From the Rhone valley a postal bus service runs from Brig to Gletsch, where it is possible to continue over either the Grimsel or Furka. For the motorist it is useful to know that in case of bad weather, when the passes can be temporarily closed, an alternative route to Lucerne from Göschenen via Altdorf lies along the E side of Lake Lucerne; a long but sure way.

Maps and Guidebooks

This guidebook is designed for use with the Swiss Federal maps (LK) which are very accurate and easy to follow. Till quite recently the largest scale maps generally available were on a scale of 1:50,000, but now slowly appearing are those of 1:25,000, of an excellence in revealing fine intricate detail which is unsurpassed. They are invaluable.

The maps required for this guide are:—

255	Sustenpass	1:50,000
1231	Urseren	1:25,000
1211	Meiental	1:25,000

These maps are available from Alpina Technica Services, 1 Meadow Close, Goring, Reading, Berkshire, RG8 0AP, England.

Two SAC guidebooks in German are available for the area, but the first vol. is now out of date.

SAC: *Urner Alpen*, Vol II, 1952
Revised edition – *Urner Alpen West*, 1966

Altitudes and Nomenclature

All measurements and altitudes are expressed in the metric system and the latter taken from the LK. Where there is no name or height given on the map it has usually been taken from a continental publication or gained by personal knowledge. Where there are two spellings of place names reference is made to both the old and new to avoid confusion.

Orientation

Whenever possible the directions 'left' and 'right' have been used in the sense of direction of the climber – ascent, descent, traverse of slope. Natural mtn. features such as glaciers, couloirs and rivers are identified by the direction of flow, i.e. downwards. In case of doubt the direction is confirmed by an abbreviated compass point.

Huts and Camping

Many huts such as the Gelmer and Bergsee are modern and comfortable, others far less so. All belong to the SAC, and all must be approached on foot. The same rules of hut life apply as in any other district and when a warden is resident this is indicated in the text.

Unlike many areas there are often splendid and unobtrusive camp sites within the vicinity of the hut; and in the rocky mtns. good bivouac sites can be found among boulders.

Equipment

Commonsense should determine what equipment is necessary when contemplating a climb, depending on difficulty and the terrain to be covered. Enough has been said about the use of helmets and this must remain the choice of the individual. Bearing in mind the extensive glaciation of the region, snow/ice equipment should be taken as a rule.

Language and Currency

German is spoken throughout the region but very little French or English. It is very useful to have some knowledge of German rather than to expect the resident people to address you in English.

As the area is wholly in Switzerland there are no currency complications. Travellers cheques can be useful but they can also be a nuisance, involving descents into the valley to find a bank open at an appropriate time. Good exchange facilities exist in Meiringen, Andermatt and Göschenen, but difficulties will be encountered elsewhere.

Rate of exchange at April, 1969: £1=SF.10.50 (SF.1.00= 1s. 11d). $1.00=SF.4.30 (SF.1.00=24 cents).

Grading

In accordance with the UIAA classification system, the grading of climbs is numerical from I to VI and A1, A2, A3 and A4 for artificial, with the letter 'e' to denote the use of expansion bolts (i.e. A4e). Grade I is the easiest and VI the hardest. Variations of difficulty are denoted by + and − signs; plus is above the normal rating and minus below (i.e. VI−/VI/VI+). For the expert climber only variations above grade IV will really matter, but these sub-divisions of difficulty should be equally helpful in the lower grades for the average climber. It must be emphasised that the grade of climb is determined not only by pure technical difficulties but also by objective dangers and length.

For a comparison with the six main grades, the following adjectives are normally employed at present (with the British system in parentheses):—

I	Easy (easy)
II	Moderate (moderate/moderately difficult)
III	Moderately difficult (difficult/very difficult)
IV	Difficult (severe)
V	Very difficult (very severe)
VI	Extremely difficult (hard very severe and upwards)

Some or all of the following attributes in technical climbing, as applicable, appear in route descriptions: climbs exposed or poorly protected; often or mostly overhanging; friction climbing; objective dangers; bad rock; complicated route finding; retreat difficult; pitch lengths where known; rock type; climatic considerations; bivouac places; pegs and aids necessary; length of climb; route times; quality and character of route.

Valley Bases

All towns and villages mentioned below are interconnected by an efficient postal bus service. Time tables can be obtained locally, or from Swiss National Tourist offices in capital cities outside Switzerland.

Innertkirchen 622m. A small attractive village conveniently situated at the foot of both the Grimsel and Susten passes. Reasonable accommodation and good for supplies, but too low to be used as a climbing base.

Guttannen 1049m. A very pleasant small village just before the main rise to the Grimsel pass. One hotel with varied accommodation; and shop for provisions. A good centre for expeditions into the Tieralplistock group.

Handegg 1404m. A short distance above but considerably higher than Guttannen. Only one hotel, originally built for the famous Handegg Falls; now non-existent. Useful as a base for the Gelmer hut, but rather too low for climbing.

Grimsel Pass 2165m. Reasonably priced hotel in a wonderful situation with splendid panoramic views. A good high base for the Gerstenhörner and Nägelisgrätli.

Gletsch c.1700m. A huge sombre hotel at the S foot of the Grimsel pass. Once very popular before the marked recession of the Rhone glacier; now merely a symbol of the past. Interesting for some wild remote walks, but of little use as a climbing base.

Hotel Belvédère 2274m. A large fairly expensive hotel with a famous view of the Rhone glacier. Over half-way up the Furka pass, it is rather touristy, but very convenient for climbing on the Rhone glacier, Galenstock and Furkahorn.

Tiefenbach 2109m. A tiny village on E side of the Furka pass. Very limited accommodation; rarely used because the Albert Heim hut is so close. Poor for supplies.

Realp 1538m.; **Zumdorf** 1496m.; **Hospental** 1453m. Three villages situated low down in the Urseren valley, rather bleak and uninteresting in summer as they are really ski resorts. Provisions can be bought, but the villages are too low to be convenient climbing centres.

Andermatt   1436m.   A large popular ski resort. Plenty of shops and hotels, all fairly expensive. Good exchange facilities.

Göschenen   1101m.   A busy, somewhat unpleasant small town on the main Gotthard road. Reasonable hotels and good shops; exchange facilities. A good base for huts in the Göschener and Voralp valleys.

Wassen   916m.   A small town similar in many respects to Göschenen. Numerous hotels, often full with over night travellers on the Gotthard road. Situated at the E foot of the Susten pass.

Dörfli   1274m.;   **Färnigen**   1455m.   Two tiny villages on E side of the Susten pass. Limited accommodation and shops, and unsatisfactory as climbing bases except for the mtns. N of the road, the Sewen and Leidstock.

Stein   1863m.   The main centre on W side of the Susten pass. One good, reasonable hotel, but no shops for provisions. A good base for the Tierbergli hut and the Tierberg group generally. Unfortunately it is apt to become rather overrun with tourists during the day.

Gadmen   1205m.   A small charming village above Innertkirchen. Only really useful for climbing on the Tellistock to the NW. Limited in accommodation and shops.

Gelmer Hut   2412m.

Situated below the moraine of the Dietcher glacier with a splendid view of the Gelmerhörner. Built in 1926, belongs to the Section Brugg, SAC. Thoroughly modernised in the 1960s: with its own electrical generator it is the warmest and most comfortable hut in this part of the Alps. Places for 50 and usually a hut keeper in summer.

1. From Künzentannlen (postal bus halt), a short distance above Handegg on the Grimsel pass, ascend a steep but clearly defined path to the Gelmersee (lake). Cross the dam wall NW, then take the path cut in the rockface above the lake; NW side. After the end of the lake go up for a short distance into the valley, Unter Dietcher (hut visible) then cross the stream E (planks) to the path on the other side. Continue up this over steep rough ground, passing an impressive waterfall to the L, and eventually reach the hut ($3\frac{1}{2}$–4h. from Künzentannlen).

Windegg Hut   1887m.

Situated S of the Windegg ridge and within a short distance of the Trift glacier. A small hut originally built in 1891 and rebuilt in 1925. Room for 12 and no hut keeper. Water can be obtained about 15m. along path to Trift hut. It belongs to the Bern Section, SAC.

2. From the Susten pass, a short distance above Innertkirchen, branch off R at pt.940m. to a small secondary road. Go along this for 300m. to a bridge (R) that crosses the Trift stream; the path for the hut starts here. Follow it, clearly marked all the way to hut; steep in final stages (3–4h. from road).

Trift Hut   2520m.

A finely situated hut, wild and isolated, overlooking the Trift glacier basin and surrounding peaks. It is not easy to reach and should only be attempted by climbers not walkers. In bad weather the correct route is difficult to find. Built in 1864, and rebuilt on a new site in 1947. Places for 45, usually no hut keeper. It is the property of the Bern Section SAC.

3. From the Windegg hut follow the path SE to a cairn marking the descent to Trift glacier. Descend for 70m. over good, slabby rock, then down a crack in a series of steep rock steps. Continue down for a further 100m. over steep scree and moraine to the glacier. Cross this easily (dry) SE towards the narrow mouth of the Zwischen Tierbergen and the R-hand (S) corner. Go up R of the stream (NE) towards the Z. Tierbergen glacier to reach a huge distinct block with red hut markings. Now follow the hut path for about 100m. (path ceases), up steep grass for a few m., then rejoin the path which is followed to the top level of the rock buttress falling to glacier. The track now continues over a steep rocky section with red flashes, then goes horizontally over rocky slabs; the 'Tältiplatten'. After this cross a small stream (L), go up a chimney-like rock pitch then a final 150–200m. to hut (2½–3h. from Windegg hut).

Tierbergli Hut   2797m.
A grand position amid impressive glacier scenery, and within easy reach of the Susten pass. Care should be taken on the final stretch which is steep and over snow. Built in 1942, 65 places, belongs to the Baselland Section, SAC. Hut keeper in summer. During the latter part of the 1968 season the hut was temporarily closed for renovation.

4. From the Hotel Stein glacier on the Susten pass cross the stream (bridge) and follow the good path to pt. 2427m.; the rognon in the Stein and Steinlimmi glaciers. From here climb the buttress in a series of zigzags to hut, usually over snow (3h. from Stein).

Albert Heim Hut
A popular hut standing in a pronounced position on a large rocky outcrop. Built in 1918, and rebuilt in 1937. Places for 50, belongs to the SAC Section Uto. There is usually a hut keeper at weekends and in mid-summer.

5. From Realp take the path rising steeply past pt.1829m. (NW); easy to follow. Now go up by Lochberg and Sass, pt. 2305m., and through the deep ravine between a large rock buttress (L), with a hut on top, and the Sunnig Berg (R); then climb up and round to S and so reach hut (3–3½h.).

6. From Tiefenbach on the Furka pass; a small village above Realp, 2109m. Most parties take this route; much shorter and more pleasant (several laybys on road for cars). From here follow an easy and unexacting path leading to hut (N) (1–1½h. from road).

Bergsee Hut 2370m.
A new hut completed in 1966; N of the Göscheneralpsee and S of the Bergseeschijen. Ideally situated for climbs in this group which were always difficult to reach in the past. Belongs to the Section Angenstein, SAC, places for 15. Hut keeper in summer.

7. From restaurant by the dam wall of the Göscheneralpsee follow the clearly defined path (N) to hut in about 2h. A daily postal bus service runs from Göschenen to the restaurant.

Kehlenalp Hut 2350m.
Situated at the head of the Göschener Tal amid an impressive cirque of great peaks. Built in 1903 and enlarged in 1926, places for 90. Property of the Section Aarau, SAC. Hut keeper sometimes present.

8. From the dam wall of the Göscheneralpsee follow the path along N side of lake; this drops to the valley beyond lake. Now continue along the path on the N side of the Chelenreuss (stream), past several cairns to pt.2127.8m. and a large cairn. This is directly below the hut; now bear R (NW) and climb steeply to hut (2½–3h. from dam).

Damma Hut 2440m.
A small, pleasant hut with a splendid view of the Dammastock group and its surrounding glaciers. Built in 1915; renovated and enlarged in 1962 to sleep 30. Belongs to the Pilatus Section, SAC; usually no hut keeper.

9. From the restaurant by the Göscheneralpsee cross the dam wall and take the path rising steeply on S side of the lake. Continue high above the lake then descend and cross the Dammareuss (stream). After a short distance turn sharp L, then follow the path SW. Finally climb steeply N to hut. It is also possible to join the path at a pt. after the Dammareuss by cutting up SE from the Kehlenalp hut path immediately after the lake.

Voralp Hut   2126m.

A small hut at head of the Voralptal below the SW walls of the Fleckistock and Winterberg. A pleasant easy walk through an unspoilt valley. Built in 1891, renovated in 1959. Room for 30. Usually no hut keeper. Property of the Section Uto, SAC.

10. From Göschenen follow road to second hairpin bend after the tiny village of Wiggen. Cross the Voralpreuss (stream) R then follow the path up past Mittwald, 1654m., Hörefelli, 1781m. and Bodmen, 1903m. to the Voralp hut (2½h. from the hairpin bend, 4h. from Göschenen).

Salbit Hut   2105m.

The hut is ideally situated for practically all routes on the Salbitschijen and its adjacent pts. and ridges, and within easy reach of Göschenen. Property of the Lindenberg Section, SAC; places for 50 with warden in summer.

11. From Göschenen, coming from Wassen take the road to the R, just before the bridge in the centre of the town (the main road over the bridge leads via the Gotthard pass to Andermatt). Continue along the road in the Göschener Tal to the smal village of Abfrutt. Go R beside the chapel, then climb a zigzag path to Regliberg; or go further along the road to just beyond Ulmi to pt. 1195m., and from here bear R and climb steeply through the wood to Regliberg. Both paths are signposted; the latter is somewhat more direct. Now follow the path through Trögen to hut (2½–3h.).

  Abfrutt is a postal bus stop and Ulmi is at request.

The small cable car above the road should not be used by climbers; it is for the use of the hut keeper and villagers of Regliberg for transportation of goods. Those who use it to save their legs do so at their own risk.

PART I

TIERALPLISTOCK GROUP

This forms the most westerly group in the guide, bounded on the E by the Dammastock–Tierberg ridge and the icefields of the Trift and Rhone glaciers, and on the W by the Hasli valley and Grimsel pass. It is comprised of a long mtn. ridge running S to N for about 14km.; intersected by numerous useful passes. The Nägelisgratli and Gerstenhörner mark the most southerly point, the Mährenhorn and Benzlauistock the most northerly.

The western aspect is one of a wild rocky wilderness, that from the E of more gentle rotund snow peaks. Most of the mtns. offer interesting easy rock ridges or scrambles with relatively little glacier work, especially from the Hasli valley. From the Trift and Rhone glaciers the routes are of a far more serious nature, requiring experience in glacier travel. The whole area is scenically beautiful with the mtns. forming excellent viewpoints. It is ideal for the true mtn. enthusiast, both climber and walker, and is perfect for the less able or experienced mountaineer or for a first season.

The precipitous towers of the Gelmerhörner above Handegg are an exception, forming a climbing paradise for the rock specialist. The rock is of excellent Aare granite and affords a wonderful selection of first class routes in nearly all degrees of difficulty; steep and exposed.

Three mtn. huts serve the area, the Windegg, Trift and Gelmer; the latter being the most modern, up to date and popular.

BLATTENSTOCK   1849.3m.

The most northerly pt. of the Tieralplistock group. An easy mtn. of low altitude with no technical climbing, but interesting for the mtn. walker and a good view pt.

West Side (from Alp Blatten).

12. From Innertkirchen follow the Grimsel road to pt. 649m. Take the path (E), rising slightly and parallel to the road till above Aelauenen. Cross a small stream, then recross it again.

After a short distance the path zigzags steeply to Alp Blatten. Continue to Blatten, pt. 1599m., then W-wards to the top (3–4 h.).

A descent can be made by following the track on E side through Alp Speicherberg to the Nessental. This is a little above Mühletal, itself only a short distance from Innertkirchen (2½h.). Not recommended for ascent; poor path, long and tedious.

BENZLAUISTOCK   2530m.

North-East Ridge. *The higher SE neighbour of the Blattenstock. A good view pt., an interesting and worthwhile expedition for the mtn. walker. More serious than the Blattenstock.*

13. Follow Route 12 to Blatten, pt.1599m., then go SE to Schnoss, pt.1782m. below the Männlisegg. The path now bears more SW to the Alp Benzlaui, 1844m. Climb beside the Benzlaui stream on its L side to the Benzlaui lakes, pt.2179m. Now scramble over scree to reach a saddle NE of the summit. From here follow the ridge easily to the top (5½–6h.). More often used as a descent route (see 14).

West-North-West Ridge. *Interesting and easy on the ridge, but tedious from Blatten up to Stiergrind. A traverse of this mtn. is recommended for those with enough energy. I. The route from Nessental over Alp Speicherberg is far too steep, overgrown and tedious to be recommended.*

14. Follow Route 12 to Blatten, pt.1599m. Now bear NE over steep grass, bushes and undergrowth to Stiergrind, then follow the ridge easily to summit (4½h.).

GRAUSTOCK   2690m.
BRUNNENSTOCK   2493m.

East-South-East traversing ridge. *An easy interesting climb, but a long approach and descent to the valley. I.*

15. From Benzlaui Alp (Route 13) climb scree to the saddle between the Benzlauistock and pt.2384m. Now follow the ridge (ESE) easily to the Brunnenstock and continue in the same direction to the Graustock. From the E summit descend a series of large but straightforward slabs to a distinct saddle (E), then down to the Alp Holzhaus. Descend to the Wannisbordsee (lake), pt.2104m. (S). Continue down through Wannisbord to small bridge and a path. Follow this path W round the corner of the Hohmadstock S ridge, passing pt. 2129m. to reach Benzlauialp (Innertkirchen–Benzlauialp, 3–3½h. Benzlauialp–Brunnenstock–Graustock, 2½h. Graustock-Holzhausalp 1h. At least 8h. for round trip).

MÄHRENHORN   2922.6m.

The highest and most important mtn. in this group NW of the Furtwangsattel. The W ridge is fairly difficult and long and is the most interesting. Descent is usually by the E ridge to Holzhaus Alp. An excellent viewpoint. First ascent: J. J. Schweizer with two sons and two local herdsmen from Steinhaus Alp, 1821.

East Ridge. *An easy scramble, usually used for descent.* I.

16. From Holzhaus Alp, NE of Guttannen, climb past the Wannisbordsee, then up grass and scree to the saddle between the E and main summit. Now follow the ridge easily to top. A variant is sometimes possible on the SE side when there is an accumulation of old snow. This can also be used as a fas descent (2–2½h. from Holzhaus Alp).

West Ridge. *By far the most interesting route on the mtn.* II.

17. From Holzhaus Alp climb past the Wannisbordsee then up easily to the saddle E of the Graustock. From here follow the W ridge directly to summit (3–3½h. from Holzhaus Alp).

By Windegg and Stotziggrates. *An easy route, scenically beautiful and in wild surroundings.* I.

18. From the Windegg hut go over the ridge of the Windegg to pt.2179m. Now descend S side of the Windegghorn and rise along S side of the Stotziggrates to reach pt.2647m. Now ascend snow to the E summit, then follow E ridge to the main peak (3½h. from hut).

North Ridge. *An easy route, with splendid views of the Gadmental and Gadmenfluh, but quite long and tiring.* I.

19. From the Windegg hut go NW over scree, snow and rock to Schonhubel. Cross snow to the ridge and reach it without difficulty about 100m. below pt. 2486m. Follow it easily to summit (4–5h. from hut).

The N ridge at pt.2486m. may also be reached from the Nessental via Lauband Zum See, but this is too long to be popular, involving an ascent of nearly 2000m.

WEISSE SCHIJEN   c.2800m.

Three distinct rock towers on the N ridge running from the Furtwangsattel, to the Mährenhorn. The two most northerly towers offer short climbs (cracks, III) on the N side, with a 35m. free abseil down the E wall of the middle tower. Too far from the valley to attract many climbers. First ascent: W. Gysin and O. Lienhard, 28 July, 1937.

FURTWANGSATTEL   2561m.

An interesting and popular pass. The best and shortest route from Guttannen to the Windegg hut and down to Gadmen via the Rindertal and Shattigtrifttäli. Good views of the Bernese Alps.

20. From Guttannen cross the bridge over the Aare (off the main road, L by Hotel Baren) and follow path to the open meadow at Weisstannen, 1492m. Bear R and pass round the edge of the wood to rejoin a good track leading to bridge over the Hostett stream. Cross this and follow track to the high cattle station of Alp Holzhaus. Bear R by the sheds, then directly up into the Rindertal, scree, steep grass and old snow. Climb direct, the path becomes vague, then bear R (path) to a small subsidiary ridge. Cross this then go up to the pass above on L (3½–4h.).

Descent to Windegg hut.

21. From the pass descend directly over rock, scree and snow to the head of the Schattigtrifttäli. Descend this valley on the L side below the Stotziggrates to small lake at pt. 2272m. Now bear L to avoid the steep zone of the Gleckplatten, to reach pt. 2179m.; large cairn. Go along the ridge of the Windegg and join the hut path by pt. 1915m. (1½–2h.).

STEINHAUSHORN   3120m.

An easy mtn. from all sides but impressive looking and well worth climbing. One of the most interesting routes is a traverse from the Kilchlistock, combining Routes 29 or 30/22. First ascent: J. Frey, 1815.

South-East Ridge. *A short interesting route.* I. *Diagram, p.27.*

22. From the saddle N of the Kilchlistock (Route 31) follow the ridge easily to summit (30 min. from saddle).

West-South-West Ridge. *An easy ridge, not really recommended, being too loose and also too long from Guttannen.* I. *Diagram, p.27.*

23. From Alp Steinhaus climb the scree called Gummi to pt. 2612m. Now follow the easy but broken ridge to summit (3½h. from Alp Steinhaus).

West Side. *A better and more interesting route than the WSW ridge.* I. *Diagram, p.27.*

24. From Alp Steinhaus climb straight up steep grass and scree below Stöckli, pt. 2424m. to pt. 2559m. Climb an easy couloir to pt. 3023m. on the NW ridge, pleasant when filled with snow. Now follow Route 27 to summit (2½h. from Alp Steinhaus). A shorter, easier couloir also leads to pt. 2935.6m.

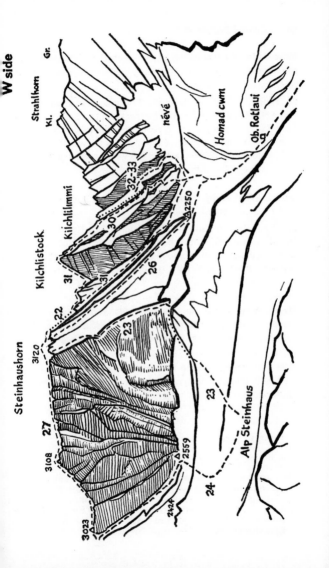

W side

Strahlhorn

Gr.

Kl.

névé

Homad cwm

Ob. Rotlaui

Kilchlilmmi

32-33

30

31

31

26

2250

Kilchlistock.

22

23

Steinhaushorn

3/20

27

23

3108

Alp Steinhaus

3023

2424

2559

24

East Side. *An interesting glacier expedition in beautiful surroundings, technically easy but badly crevassed in places. A good route for ski mountaineering.*

25. From the Trift hut cross the Trift glacier at c.2400m., then climb NW towards pt.2827m., the rocks of the Sackgrätli. Now bear SW over the glacier to reach the summit. The saddle N of the Kilchilistock can be reached easily anywhere from here. This detour to pt.2827m. avoids the worst crevasses in centre of the glacier (2–3h.).

South-West Ridge. *An easy route, one of the most straightforward on the mtn. I. Diagram, p.27.*

26. From Ober Rotlaui, pt.1922m. climb NE by Hohmad into the Steinhaushorn–Ofenhorn hollow, to pt.2250m. Now climb the distinct rib immediately above to join the summit ridge a short distance from top. Finally, go up the SE ridge (1½–2h. from Ober Rotlaui).

North-West Ridge. *An interesting high level ridge, but far too loose in places to be recommended. II. First ascent: G. Studer with Bauman and Weissenfluh, 9 August, 1841. Diagram, p.27.*

27. From the Furtwangsattel follow the ridge over pts.2935-6-3023 and 3108m., thence to summit. Whenever possible it is best and quickest to use snow on the N side (6–7h. from Guttannen).

KILCHLISTOCK   3114m.

The immediate SE neighbour of the Steinhaushorn. A fine impressive peak with a number of short interesting climbs. First ascent: A. Hoffman-Burkhardt with U. Lauener and A. Weissenfluh, 14 July, 1865 (same day as the Matterhorn) by Trift glacier and Sacktäli. First ascent from Guttannen: Baumgartner, Kocher and Bremond with von Bergen, Tännler, Moor and Stähli, 7 September, 1888. First traverse N to S: E. Burckhardt, 1891.

South-East Side. *An easy and fairly interesting route.* I.

28. From the Kilchilimmi (Routes 32/33) climb an obvious broad and easy snow couloir nearly to the top. Finally over easy rocks to summit (1h.).

East Ridge. *A good route, one of the most interesting on the mtn.; scenically fine.* I/III.

29. Get on to the ridge on the S side from Kilchlilimmi without difficulty then follow the crest with interesting and varied climbing to top (1h. from start of ridge).

South-West Edge. *A fine climb, the most direct line on the mtn. Recommended.* III+. *First ascent: H. Etter and E. Reiss, October, 1945. Diagram, p.27.*

30. Follow Route 32 to the rock terrace, then climb the difficult and exposed *kante* on excellent rock to summit. The most difficult problem, a large slabby buttress, is turned on the L side by a chimney/crack (1–2h. from start).

North Saddle and North Side. *The deepest gap in ridge between Kilchlistock and Steinhaushorn. One of the longest routes. Not too difficult and quite interesting.* II/III. *Diagram, p.27.*

31. Follow Route 32 to SW wall of the Kilchlistock. Now work L along foot of wall to reach the distinct couloir rising directly to the saddle above. Climb diagonally across the foot of this couloir (do not climb it, dangerous stonefall) and at c.2400m. get on to and climb the N bordering rocks to reach the SE ridge of the Steinhaushorn. Now descend the ridge (S) for a short distance to the deep saddle. From here climb directly to summit (3½–4h.).

KILCHLILIMMI 2942m.

A saddle between the Kl. Strahlhorn (3085m.) and the Kilchlistock (3114m.). As a pass from Rotlaui to the Trift glacier (hut) it is seldom used, preference being given to the route over the Furtwangsattel (20). The latter is decidedly easier with fewer route finding problems and little glacier work. There are two routes from the Hohmad névé; there can be no special preference but Route 33 up the couloir is shorter and more direct.

By SW side of the Kilchlistock. *Diagram, p.27.*

32. From Ober Rotlaui (1922m.) climb scree and grass through Hohmad then over snow to foot of the Kilchlistock SW wall. From the summit two very steep gullies run down to a snow cone at the foot of the wall. Go up scree cone W of these gullies, then up easy grassy rocks. After a short distance bear R and cross the gullies to reach the projecting corner of a conspicuous rock terrace. Cross this to its upper end, then reach the pass quickly and easily by a deep couloir (2–3h. from Hohmad névé).

By the 'Couloir' from Hohmad névé. *Diagram, p.27.*

33. From the névé go SE to foot of a narrow couloir leading directly to the pass. Climb this without difficulty to top, sometimes over snow but usually rocks. It is also possible to leave this couloir by going L to the rock terrace and joining Route 32 (1–2h. from Hohmad névé).

The couloir is the best and quickest means of descent from the Kilchlilimmi. It is also possible, just above the rock terrace, to go L over a rock rib to reach another couloir and descend its easy snow quickly to Hohmad (30 min.).

MITTAGFLUH   c.1865m.

This is merely a low truncated spur descending E from the Ofenhorn; easily recognised from Guttannen.

South Edge. *A short route, usually climbed in the Spring or when bad weather rules out higher climbs. IV/V, c.200m. First ascent: E. Rufibach and H. Streich, 13 October, 1963.*

34. Leave the Grimsel road by the Tschingel bridge at pt.1146m., then go NE to foot of the *kante* at pt.1456m. Start somewhat to the R, then climb the edge more or less direct, varying L or R according to difficulties till about 60m. below summit. Now follow a well-defined crack leading R off the crest for about 40m., up to an overhang. Climb this on its L side, then return to the *kante*. The difficulties soon end, but keep on the crest to top (2–3h.).

Descent.

35. Traverse NE through Flachsgarten to pt.1940m.; do not attempt to move down before this pt. Now either descend directly through Rotlaui over rough ground or cross N to Ober Rotlaui, 1922m. to join a path down (2–2½h.). It is not possible to descend on S side (very steep and dangerous).

GWÄCHTENHORN 3214.5m.

One of the highest mtns. in this group. No real technical difficulties, but a serious glacier approach on E side from the Trift hut. An excellent view pt. Very popular in winter as a ski mtn. First ascent: A. Hoffman, 13 July, 1865. Traversed a fortnight later by Gottlieb Studer, forced to bivouac beside Triftstöckli.

North-West Ridge. *The normal route from the Gelmer hut, easy and worthwhile. First ascensionist.*

36. From the Gwächtenlimmi (Route 40) follow the ridge easily to summit (4h. from Gelmer hut).

West Rib. *The most difficult route on the mtn., seldom done owing to bad stonefall. III. First ascent: E. Gasser, O. Frei and C. Pfrunder Jr., 9 August, 1928.*

37. From the Gelmer hut follow Route 40 to the Diechter glacier and climb to the foot of the most southerly summit. Follow this rib directly to the summit ridge (4h. from the hut).

South-East Ridge (from Trift glacier). *The normal route from the Trift hut. Impressive glacier scenery. Easy. A ski route.*

38. From the Trift hut cross the Trift glacier SW to pt.2511m.

at the foot of the Triftstöckli. Now climb easy but badly crevassed névé to the SE ridge and follow this to summit (4–5h. from hut).

By Unter Trift Kessel and Triftstöckli. *A good route, somewhat longer than the normal but more interesting and not so badly crevassed. A ski route.* I.

39. From the Trift hut climb S into the Unter Trift kessel, skirting bad crevasses to the R. Now climb SE, then back to the W, avoiding the large icefall, to join the middle of the Triftstöckli–Diechterhorn ridge, SW of pt.3035.3m. From here either traverse up across to the summit, or climb straight up, keeping close to the Triftstockli ridge, to pt.3148m, then up the ridge to top (4–6h. from the hut).

GWÄCHTENLIMMI   c.3100m.

A small pass not marked by LK, between the Gwächtenhorn (3214.5 m.) and Gross Strahlhorn (3156 m.). Popular in winter as a ski route from Gelmer hut to the Trift or Windegg huts. Easy but crevassed on Trift (E) side.

From Gelmer hut.

40. Go up N through Ob. Diechter and pass pt.2697m. on the R (E), then climb to the Diechter glacier. Now trend NW up easy névé to the snowy saddle (2h. from hut).

From Trift hut.

41. Follow Routes 38 or 39 nearly to summit of the Gwächtenhorn, then bear R (N) and easily reach pass (3–4h. from hut).

GROSS STRAHLHORN   3156m.

An easy mtn., best combined with a traverse to the Kl. Strahlhorn (Route 43), thence to the Kilchlistock (Route 44). Both Strahlhorns are popular with crystal and mineral hunters. Excellent view pt. First traverse of mtn.: H. A. Weber with H Konig and Nussberger, July, 1901.

From Gwächtenlimmi by South-East Ridge. I.

42. From this pass (Route 40) follow the ridge easily to top (10–15 min.).

KLEIN STRAHLHORN   3085m.

The slightly lower neighbour of the Gross. The two ridges are easy and interesting. Can be climbed from Hohmad but this is too dangerous from stonefall to be recommended. First ascent: Paul Montandon and his wife, 16 September, 1900.

North Ridge (from Gr. Strahlhorn). *The best route on the mtn.* I.

43. Follow Route 42 to top of the Gr. Strahlhorn, then follow the N ridge without difficulty to summit (20–30 min.).

South-East Ridge (from Kilchlilimmi). *Not often done; easy, but often icy when it can become quite tricky.* I.

44. From the Kilchlilimmi (Route 32) follow the ridge easily to top (20–30 min. from pass).

OFENHORN   2948m.,   2933.9m.

The westerly peak forming the Diechter cwm above the Gelmer hut. An easy mtn. of no great interest. It is usual to traverse the two summits, then descend the NE ridge to a small saddle, thence E down to Ob. Diechter.

From the Outer Garwidilimmi. I. *Diagram, p.41.*

45. From this pass (Route 47) climb the easy slope lying between the S and SW ridges to the top (3h. from Gelmer hut).

GARWIDILIMMI   Outer (N) 2685m.   Inner (S) 2678m.

Two minor passes between the Ofenhorn and Gelmerspitzen. Not often climbed from Guttannen, but popular from the Gelmer hut for the Ofenhorn and Gelmerspitzen.

From Guttannen via Rotlauital.

46. From Ober Rotlaui go S to pt.1940m., then SW to pt 1978.7m. Now trend E through Flachsgarten, then traverse round to S, avoiding cliffs on the R to pt.2303.1m. Finally mount E through the zone of Garmidi, grass, rocks and scree, to either pass (5–6h.).

The other route from Guttannen via Tschingelmad and Scholauiberg is not recommended; steep rough ground with difficult route finding.

From Diechtertal. *Digram, p.41.*

47. From the Gelmer hut climb to Ob. Diechter, keeping to L side of the valley, then work W over scree or moraine to either pass (1½–2h.).

GELMERHÖRNER

The most impressive and popular climbing area in the Tieralplistock. The group comprises the Kl. and Gr. Gelmerhörner and the Gelmerspitzen, seven in all, forming a fine serrated ridge running from above the Gelmersee NE to the Inner Garwidilimmi. Most of the routes are fairly short, but with a good selection of grades from III to V+ with straightforward artificial of A1/A2 all on perfect rock (Aare granite). The classic route in the area is undoubtedly the traverse of the Kl. and Gr. Gelmerhörner from S to N (Route 64). Although the peaks are fairly low, the approach from the Grimsel valley is quite long and strenuous, and all climbs should be done from the comfortable Gelmer hut.

KLEIN GELMERHORN

A characteristic granite pinnacle, reminiscent of a Chamonix Aig. The most popular mtn. in this group.

South Ridge. *The classic route, short, steep, exposed and on excellent rock.* III+. *First ascent: H. A. Weber and A. Tannler, 9 July, 1901. Diagram, p.40.*

48. From the S Gelmerlücke (Route 53) follow the ridge easily at first, keeping more on the E side, then climb a series of blocks and steps to a steep section. Climb this by a steep chimney, then follow the crest delicately to below the main summit block. Bridge up an obvious detached block-like slab (separated from the main summit) and at the top make a delicate move to a small stance away from the block slab (key pitch). From here the summit needle can be quickly reached by the smooth, difficult S *kante* (room for 3–4 people only) (3–4h. from hut).

West Pillar. *A good sustained climb on excellent rock, one of the longest in the group. 350m., V and A1. First ascent: H. Tschanz, P. Allenbach and E. Frudli, 1963.*

49. From the Gelmer hut follow Route 53 to the S Gelmerlücke. Now descend W in a couloir to foot of a series of large slabs. Traverse across foot of these to a point in line with summit. Climb directly, over increasingly steep and difficult slabs, using a system of cracks; then climb a steep wall to reach a grassy hollow. Now climb a dièdre and reach the edge of the pillar. Go R and up the next dièdre (several pegs), then up a steep wall to a good peg. Pendule traverse R to a distinct crack; good stance. Climb this crack direct (pegs and wedges), then go R to below an overhang; good belay. Climb the overhang and continue up the crack above which leads L to a large stance. The last section of the climb is now divided into two steep sections. Climb the first on the R, the second on L and by a dièdre. Continue to foot of summit block; move L and join Route 48 by the S ridge (6–7h.).

North-East Wall. *A good route, steep and exposed on excellent rock. V–. First ascent: H. Baumgartner and H. Wäffler, 18 September, 1938. Diagram, p.40.*

50. From the Gelmersattel (Route 56) climb a chimney in the N edge to below a very steep section. Now take a crack on the L which leads to a small but obvious outcrop. From this abseil for 8–10m. and swing across to a small stance. Follow an obvious crack in the wall, as far as a projecting chockstone, which bars the way. Traverse R for 2m., then take a thin crack which soon widens and has good holds. Turn a large block on its L side, then continue to trend L towards the summit block and join Route 48 (3–4h.).

South-East Pillar. *A fine interesting climb, the hardest on the mtn. Good rock. Pegs and wedges should be taken, 250m., V+, A1–A2. First ascent: P. Arigoni and E. Friedli, 1964. Diagram, p.40.*

51. From the Gelmersattel (Route 56) between the two Gelmerhörner, a deep couloir drops in the direction of the Gelmersee. Below the sattel and to the L of this couloir rises the steep buttress of the SE pillar. The pillar is cut throughout its height by a crack, up which the route lies.

From the couloir (Route 56) slant L for about three rope-lengths to foot of the pillar. Climb a wide crack to below a small roof; peg stance. Continue direct over the roof (wedges) and the crack above to a good stance. Follow two parallel cracks which narrow to a single thin crack beneath a large overhang; peg stance. Climb the overhang and the crack above which merges into the next wall. Make a tricky move R to reach a small niche with a good stance about 2m. above. From here slant R at first, then climb steep rocks direct to a shoulder on S ridge; follow this to summit (Route 48) (6–8h.).

Descent by N ridge to Gelmersattel.
52. From the summit block abseil down the first steep wall, and continue down to edge of a large slab. Abseil down this to the saddle below. From here follow Route 56 to the Gelmer hut. A good long rope is very useful for this steep descent.

SOUTH GELMERLÜCKE

A deep gap in the ridge S of the Kl. Gelmerhorn and N of pt.2419m. The usual approach is from the Gelmer hut via Mittel Diechter. For an easy and frequented route it gives a false impression of difficulty and danger. Nevertheless if in doubt a party should have no hesitation in using the rope, for a slip here would be fatal. I/II.

53. From the Gelmer hut descend scree to Mittel Diechter and cross the stream above the waterfall. Now traverse over easy slabs and narrow grassy ledges. Pass the two distinct gullies coming down from the N Gelmerlücke and Gelmersattel, then rise to meet the third gully descending from the S Gelmerlücke. Usually faint tracks give a fair indication of the way. Climb this gully without difficulty to the lücke (1½–2h.). *Diagram, p.40.*

West Side from Gelmersee.

Nowhere difficult but steep and complicated, demanding a fair knowledge of route finding and how to deal with potentially dangerous ground. Not recommended. I/II.

54. From pt.1854m. at the NE end of the Gelmersee, move back and round to the SW, then N to below pt.2451m., the extreme S end of the Gelmer ridge. Now move N, keeping to W side of the Gelmer ridge, across a series of steep gullies to reach a large scree or snow-filled cwm immediately W of and below the Kl. and Gr. Gelmerhörner. Climb an obvious wide chimney to the S Gelmerlücke (2–3h.).

GELMERSATTEL

The deep gap in ridge between the Kl. and Gr. Gelmerhörner.

From Kl. Gelmerhorn. *Diagram, p.40.*

55. One of the most popular and frequented routes by abseiling down the N ridge (Route 52).

From Gelmer hut. *Not used much, as most parties traverse from the Kl. Gelmerhorn. Nowhere really difficult but care should be taken.* I/II. *Diagram, p.40.*

56. From the Gelmer hut follow Route 53 to where it meets the couloir descending from the Gelmersattel. Follow this, fairly steep in places but not difficult, to sattel (1½–2h.).

GROSS GELMERHORN   2630m.

The higher but less spectacular neighbour of the Klein. The classic and most popular climbs are from the Gelmersattel in conjunction with a traverse from the Kl. From the sattel there are three main variations.

Var. I. *The easiest and least interesting.* I. *Diagram, p.40.*

57. From the sattel (Routes 48/55) traverse on to the W flank, and follow a small ridge to summit (30 min. from sattel).

Var. II. *A short interesting climb, harder than Var. I.* I/II. *Diagram, p.40.*

58. From the sattel go out to a horizontal grassy ledge on E wall. From here climb a steep smooth slab and cracks to a narrow ledge above the first section. Go along this ledge to the S ridge which is climbed without difficulty to top (1h. from sattel).

Var. III. *The most difficult and interesting route.* IV/V. *First ascent : A. Roch, F. L'Orsa and A. Dunant, 30 June, 1928. Diagram, p.40.*

59. From the sattel move a little R (E) to the foot of a wall. Climb slabs on good holds to a rocky ridge edge above. Now either climb a steep slab direct, using a twisting crack (V), then move easily along a ridge to summit; or from the ridge edge cross to a narrow ledge, and follow it, with difficulty below an overhang, then up steeply on the W wall. At the end of the ledge move delicately into a chimney which rises towards the S ridge. At the top of the chimney move delicately round an overhang and make a tricky move to reach the ridge crest; or climb steeply L, then make a pendule down to the ridge, which is followed easily to top (1–2h. from the sattel).

West Pillar. *A short, quite difficult route on good rock.* IV/V. *First ascent : W. Stähli and E. Freidli, 1963.*

60. From the S Gelmerlücke descend W in a couloir, then traverse N easily over a series of large impressive slabs to the foot of the pillar. Climb a series of cracks leading to a marked dièdre L of the pillar edge. Climb the dièdre till it is possible to exit R on to the pillar edge. Follow this to near the summit, then over blocks to top (4h. from foot of pillar).

South-West Ridge. *An interesting route in itself but the approach by Route 54 on the W side is not recommended. The best way to start is by descending from the S Gelmerlücke, but this has the disadvantage of avoiding the classic S ridge of the Kl. Gelmerhorn. II/III. First ascent: P. Montandon and K. Knicht with H. Fuhrer and K. Streun, 2 June, 1902.*

61. From cwm on the W side, reached either via pt.2451m. or by descent from the S Gelmerlücke (Route 53), get easily on to the SW ridge. Follow the ridge to the most difficult section near the top, which can be climbed (III) or avoided easily on E side. Above this the crest leads easily to summit (1½–2h. from start).

East Couloir and North Ridge (from N Gelmerlücke). *An easy climb, nearly always used as a descent route. I/II. First ascent: G. Hasler, 27 July, 1904. Diagram, p.40.*

62. From the Gelmer hut descend to Mittel Diechter and cross the stream. Ascend the steep gully rising to the deep gap between Gelmerspitzen VII and VI; the smooth white slabs of Gelmerspitze VI lie immediately to the R. At about mid-height, before the gully becomes very steep, slant L across a wide grassy terrace, usually a faint track, then down slightly to join the gully running down from the N Gelmerlücke. Climb this to top, then traverse on the W side over scree and easy rocks. Continue up a minor ridge to join the main N ridge, and follow this easily to summit (2–3h. from hut).

East Wall. *A fairly easy route; no real merit. It is not as straight-forward as 62 for descending, but is used as such. I/II. First ascent: G. Troog, H. Winzeler and O. Frei, 23 June, 1928. Diagram, p.40.*

63. Follow Route 62 to the gully coming down from the N Gelmerlücke. Now climb diagonally L across the E wall to reach

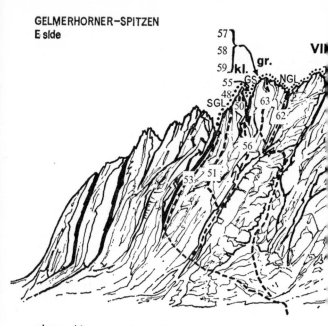

GELMERHORNER–SPITZEN
E side

57 58 59 kl. gr. VI
55 GS NGL
48 SGL 50 63 62
56
53 51

a large chimney crack, parallel to the gully. Climb this without
difficulty. At the top slant L over slabs and short, rocky steps
and ledges to top (2½–3h. from hut).

GELMERSPITZEN

These are seven prominent tower-like peaks running from the
N Gelmerlücke to Outer Garwidilimmi. Good climbs can be
had on the W and E walls, but the best route is perhaps the
complete traverse from S to N. First traverse: Helene Kuntze
with Joseph Lochmatter and a porter, 25 September, 1902.

South-North Traverse. *N Gelmerlücke to Outer Garwidilimmi.
An excellent climb on good rock; fairly sustained for the first
three peaks; it then becomes progressively easier. You can leave
the ridge at several points towards N end.* III. *Diagram, above.*

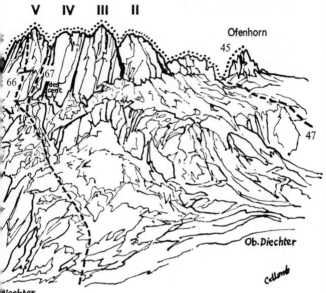

V IV III II

Ofenhorn

45

66 67 descent

47

Ob. Diechter

cellents

Diechter

64. *Gelmerspitze* VII. c.2600m. From the N Gelmerlücke (62)
follow the ridge without difficulty. Climb the first rock tower
direct or avoid it on the E(R) side across steep slabs. Now either
continue on the crest or traverse below it on the W(L) side to
reach the summit. In descent climb down directly towards the
saddle (Tiefste scharte) for the first section then make at least
two abseils down a big dièdre.

   Gelmerspitze VI. c.2600m. From the saddle move on to the
E wall, then climb for 80m. over steep slabby rock to join the
ridge. Continue along this to summit block. Climb down to
three steep block-like towers, and abseil from the middle one
for about 20m. below the crest of the ridge. Follow a ledge and
avoid the large obvious rock pinnacle on the R, then return to
ridge. Continue along the ridge, either on the crest or on the W
side if necessary to avoid the main difficulties. Near the end,

abseil again on the W side for 10m., then climb down to saddle before the next peak.

Gelmerspitze V. 2695m. From the saddle traverse a short way on to the E side, then climb a wide groove for 60m. (stance at 35m.), direct to a shoulder. From here climb towards the W ridge and follow this to below the summit block; then by the S wall. Follow the ridge N, make at least two abseils, then descend the last part free.

It is possible to descend from this saddle to the Gelmer hut by gully on the E side, with a spectacular free 25m. abseil over a massive jammed block. In ascent this obstacle is avoided by a crack on the R side.

Gelmerspitze IV. c.2600m. From saddle climb the ridge and in the upper part follow a gully to the top. Traverse the crest over the two summits, then descend without difficulty to saddle below.

Gelmerspitze III. c.2700m. At first keep somewhat on E side, then pleasant easy climbing on the ridge leads to top. Descend easily to saddle below. It is possible to descend to the hut by gully on E side.

Gelmerspitze II. 2744.9m. Climb to the top without difficulty, then traverse the long serrated ridge to the Inner Garwidilimmi.

Gelmerspitze I. 2774m. From the Inner Garwidilimmi traverse the last peak and descend to the Outer Garwidilimmi. Easy but a long broken ridge with a fair amount of loose rock and rubble. From the saddle follow Route 47 to hut (9–10h.).

Traverse from North to South. *This is a far more difficult proposition than Route 64; not so popular. The opposite traverse has several advantages; doing the best towers first, a quicker start descending from the hut, and an easier finish descending to the hut. Accurate information regarding the route has not been easy to obtain; there are too many conflicting reports and vague statements. The following brief notes can only serve as a rough guide for those sufficiently interested. A party wishing to reduce the time could omit towers I, II, III and IV by climbing the gully*

leading to the saddle beside Gelmerspitze V (Routes 64/67). IV/V,
A1. *(10–11h. for complete traverse). First traverse from peak
2774m.: G. Hasler with Heinrich Fuhrer, 29 July, 1901.*

65. From the saddle N of Tower V climb to a vague terrace
which is followed L for 30m. on to the E wall. At a prominent
projecting block traverse out for a further 20m. on to the wall,
then climb a steep chimney for about 12m. (pegs) to a tiny
stance. Pendule from here across to a smooth holdless crack
and climb this for about 8m. (IV, A1).

A route description to and over Tower VI is practically
non-existent. A difficult pendule abseil is involved, and much
of the climbing is done on the W side. Tower VII can be
climbed by its dièdre (Route 64) (IV), or directly by the steep
edge of the ridge (V—). *Diagram, p.41.*

GELMERSPITZE V.

East Wall. *A good interesting route on an impressive wall.
Usually well pegged.* IV—/V—. *First ascent: A. and W. Baltzer,
12 October, 1943. Diagram, p.41.*

66. From the Gelmer hut descend across the Mittel Diechter,
then climb easily to the large grassy terrace at foot of the wall.
Go to the extreme L of this terrace, then follow a small ledge
which runs up into the wall; reach a deep groove. Climb this
towards the small saddle between the S and main summit.
Near the top bear slightly R, then steeply to the saddle. Now
go R and up a crack to summit (4h. from start).

West Pillar. *An excellent direct route over steep slabs of perfect
rock. A fair selection of pegs and a few wedges should be taken.
Approx. 280m.,* V—/V+, A1. *First ascent: Hans Grossen and
Hans Peter Trachsel, 4 July, 1967. Diagram, p.41.*

67. The climb follows the L-hand edge of the pillar which lies
to the R of an obvious snowy couloir rising to the saddle between
Towers V and IV.

From the Gelmer hut follow Route 47 to the Inner

Garwidilimmi, then traverse down SW below the Gelmerspitzen over easy ground to the snowy coloir. Start a few m. to the R from the foot of the pillar, and follow a system of cracks for 50m. to a platform on the pillar edge (III/IV). Move 5m. R and climb cracks in a steep 35–40m. slab (pegs) to a small stance (V+, A1). Follow a small dièdre 2m. to the R, up to a ledge, then climb a steep slab to a platform on the pillar edge (25m, V−). Go L up a grey dièdre (25m.), then R to a good stance on large blocks (35m., V).

Now follow a series of cracks for 40m. in red slabs, to a small ledge (IV+). Go 3m. R into a corner crack; climb this for 20m. (III), then get into a red dièdre (easily seen from below). Climb this to the top, then move R to a stance (20m., V). Traverse L for 15m. to regain the pillar edge (IV), then take a dièdre for 5m. (A1). Climb a further 15m. trending R to reach a good stance (IV−). Finally climb progressively easier rocks for at least 40m. to summit (III+, then II) (4–5h., 1¼h. to start from hut).

Descent. Follow Route 64 down to saddle between Towers V and IV, then descend the E gully (abseil) to the middle Diechter, thence to hut (1–2h.).

GELMERSPITZE VI.
West Pillar. *A very good route following a perfect line on excellent rock. Pegs and a few wedges are necessary. 300m., V+, A1. First ascent: Hans Grossen and Hans Peter Trachsel, 5 July, 1967.*
68. The climb starts from the L (N) side of the snowy couloir rising to saddle between Towers VI and VII, and follows the sharp crest of the pillar nearly to the top.

Follow Route 67 for a further 15–20m. down SW to reach the foot of the couloir. Go up this for about 30m. to where the rock projects into the snow, then bear L for 10m. up a steep ramp, to reach the foot of the pillar. Climb the edge of the pillar for about two rope-lengths (70m., II/III), to below a zone of grey slabs.

Go L for 10m. to a dièdre and climb this to its top; in a few m. above reach a stance on a slab (30m., IV+). Climb smooth slabs direct, then easier to a stance (20m., IV+). Continue for 40m. (IV), then climb a dièdre for 20m. (IV); distinct arch formation on pillar edge. Traverse 3m. L to the pillar edge (V+), then up for 10m. in a crack to a good stance (V+). Above, climb a smooth slab for 30m. (A1), then move L to a stance on large blocks. Now climb direct for 12m. (V) to below a series of yellow roofs slanting L. Traverse L for 15m. along a steep ledge below these overhangs to the start of a dièdre (IV). Climb for 20m. to a large stance on two large jammed blocks (V). From here trend R for 5m. (V) to the start of a ribbed yellowish-black wall. Go up this for about 25m. (V+) then more easily for 45m. to summit (II/III) (4–5h. from start).

Descent. Descend to saddle between Towers VI and VII (40m. abseil), then climb down gully on E side (20m. abseil) to the Mittel Diechter, thence to hut (2–3h.).

DIECHTERHORN   3389m.   3318m.

One of the highest and most interesting mtns. dominating the Ober Diechter cwm. Impressive rock walls when viewed from the Gelmer side, but a somewhat dull snow mtn. on the Trift (E) side. Several worthwhile routes. First ascent: H. Schwarzenbach with J. von Weissenfluh, 2 August, 1864.

South Ridge. *The easiest and shortest route, offering straight-forward snow/ice techniques.* I.

69. From Dichterlimmi (Route 73) follow the easy-angled snow ridge to summit (3h. from Gelmer hut).

North-West Ridge (from Gwächtenhorn). *An easy interesting route taking in two summits. A good round tour amid superb scenery, ascending by the Gwächtenlimmi and returning via the Diechterlimmi.* I.

70. From the Gelmer hut follow Route 40 to the Gwächtenlimmi, then continue along the ridge to the Diechterhorn (3½–4h.). Descent by Route 69.

South-West Ridge. *A good route ; an excellent combination of rock and ice, the most difficult on the mtn.* II/III. *First ascent: Carl Pfrunder and K. Keller, 30 July, 1928.*

71. From the Gelmer hut go N to pt.2391m., past the large moraine, then as soon as possible NE on to the Diechter glacier. Cross the glacier to foot of the SW ridge, easily recognised, extending furthest into the ice. Climb the rocky ridge; in the upper part take a couloir on L which leads to the main summit (3½–4h.).

North-East Flank. *A fairly long climb over the Trift glacier. Easy, but with characteristic complications of crevasses, route finding, etc. A popular ski route from Trift hut.*

72. From the Trift hut follow Route 39 to a pt. below saddle in the Triftstöckli–Diechterhorn ridge. Climb below this ridge on the S side, over névé, then as soon as possible climb to pt. 3318m. (3–4h.).

From the saddle in the Triftstöckli ridge it is possible to follow the ridge directly to summit. An interesting variation.

DIECHTERLIMMI   3215m.

A snow pass between the Tieralplistock and Diechterhorn. The easiest route from the Gelmer to Trift huts. A good winter ski route.

From Gelmer hut.

73. Follow Route 71 to the Diechter glacier, then climb NE over easy névé to the pass (2½–3h.).

From Trift hut.

74. Follow Route 39 to the Ober Trift kessel. Do not go towards the Triftstöckli ridge; slant SW to the pass, easily recognised as the deepest gap S of the Diechterhorn snow ridge of pt. 3215m. (3–4h.).

TIERALPLISTOCK 3382.7m. 3360m. 3388m.

An easy snow mtn. with three summits running NW–SE. A popular route from the Gelmer hut but seldom climbed from the Furka except in winter as a ski expedition. First traverse from pt.3382.7m.: J. Jacot, 13 August, 1864.

South Flank (from Furka). *A good glacier climb; splendid scenery.* I.

75. From the Hotel Belvédère follow Route 90 across the Rhone glacier, then continue to slant up N, keeping just E of the Hinter Gelmerhörner to Tiertäli, the S cwm of the Tieralplistock. Climb to the top of the névé, then bear L (W) and reach the snow saddle N of the Hinter Gelmerhörner, pt.3317m., then up the Alpi glacier to summit (4–5h. from the Furka).

South-West Flank. *An easy, interesting route, popular with skiers in winter.* I.

76. From the Gelmersee or Gelmer hut follow Route 81 to Bergli. Now climb NE to the Alpi glacier near the foot of a rocky rib running down from pt.3139m. Climb the glacier, keeping L (NW) of a rocky outcrop, pt.3138m., and finally over easy névé to either the middle or S summit (4h. from hut).

West Flank. *More entertaining than Route 76, affording somewhat steeper snow/ice work.* II.

77. From the Gelmer hut go E for a short distance and get on to the S tip of the Diechter glacier, then bear NE to foot of a rocky spur, pt.3088m. Now climb the steep glacier S of these rocks to reach the upper névé of the Alpi glacier. From here climb to either the middle or S summit as for Route 76. (4h.).

North-West Ridge. *A fine ridge giving an interesting, easy climb.* I.

78. From the Diechterlimmi (Route 73) follow the ridge without difficulty to summit; a mixture of rock and ice (3–4h. from hut).

North-East Ridge (from Unter Triftlimmi). *A long glacier route, not done often in summer, but a popular ski route.* I.

79. From the Unter Triftlimmi (Routes 83/84) follow the snow ridge past pt.3137.4m. easily to summit (3–4h.).

East Flank. *Another popular ski route and a pleasant glacier expedition in summer.*

80. From Hotel Belvédère (Furka) follow Route 75 up below the Tälistock 3185m. Go round its N-most rocks, then up the snowy ridge on its N side past pts.3155m. and 3215m. to summit (4–5h.).

GELMERLIMMI   c.3000m.

Not marked on LK. A series of passes from Gelmer across the Hinter Gelmerhörner to the Rhone glacier and Furka. A splendid glacier expedition in impressive surroundings. The *limmi* have been used for many years but the first tourist crossing recorded was in 1840. The route described is the best. Easy.

From Gelmersee (SE side).

81. From SE side of the lake go N of Tälti, a distinct rocky cwm; bear R (E) and go up grass and scree to Bergli, then bear slightly SE to pt.2541m. (just below the rocks). Now climb the easy Gelmer glacier (few crevasses) to either of two distinct saddles in the ridge, N or S of pt.3100m.

Descend easy névé and rocks to the Rhone glacier which is followed without difficulty to pt.2380m. (Route 90), thence to Hotel Belvédère (5–6h.).

From Gelmer hut via Alpi. *It is possible to join Route 81 without descending to the Gelmersee.*

82. From the hut go E for a short way, then S to reach a large terrace which is followed up to pt.2598.4m.; then go round to a large gully. Now climb for about 50–60m. over steep rocky

steps to reach a gap in the ridge which runs down from pt.
2731m. Descend a few m. on steep scree in a gully to reach
Alpi. From here traverse E, then S, crossing two small streams
to Bergli to join Route 81 (1–1½h.).

OBER TRIFTLIMMI   3285m.

UNTER TRIFTLIMMI   c.3080m.

Two remote glacier passes connecting the Furka to the Trift
hut and Gadmen Tal. Although long and high they have been
used by local people for several generations. During the war
with France in 1789, the inhabitants of Gadmen fled from the
French across the Triftlimmi to the safety of Furka and the
Valais. They are now very popular in winter as a ski tour. I.
First tourist crossing: Gottlieb Studer, 5 August, 1839.

From Trift hut.

83. From the hut go a short distance E then S and up into the
Unter Trift kessel. Now continue in the same direction, avoiding the icefall to the R (W) to reach the Ober Trift kessel
(crevasses). From here go S to the Unter Triftlimmi (2½h.) or
SW to the Ober Triftlimmi (3h.); the latter is slightly steeper.

From Grimsel Pass.

84. From the top of the pass follow Route 90 over the
Nägelisgrätli to the Rhone glacier. Cross the glacier (NE)
easy and dry, to pt.2769m. a foot of the W side of the Galenstock. Now continue rising N over névé to the Unter Triftlimmi
or NE to the Ober Triftlimmi. For the latter pass avoid going
too far L (W) towards pt.3261m. (bad crevasses) but contour
more to R (4–5h.).

From Hotel Belvédère or Furka.

85. From the hotel follow a footpath N to pt.2580m. then
continue along the edge of the glacier to pt.2769m. to join
Route 84 (2½–3h.).

GERSTENHÖRNER

This mtn. consists of a long ridge running S–N with three principal summits; Vorder, 3186.6m., Mittler 3184m. and Hinter 3172.6m. None of them are difficult but they are rewarding view pts. They serve as an excellent training area for elementary route finding on Alpine terrain. The most interesting route is the traverse of all three tops. First tourist ascent: Gottleib Studer, 1856.

East Flank. *An easy interesting route amid magnificent glacier scenery.* I.

86. Follow Route 90 over the Nägelisgrätli, up to the Grätlisee (small lake), then go NE, up past the 2800m. contour on to the névé above rocks at pt.2686m. From here it is possible to reach the saddle between the Vorder and Mittler, or by going further N the saddle between the latter and the Hinter. From either saddle climb any of these summits without difficulty along their respective ridges (3½–4h.).

South-West Ridge (Vorder). *A short, fairly interesting route; can be done easily from the Grimsel pass. The best route for the start of the traverse; no difficulties.* I.

87. Follow Route 90 nearly as far as the Grätlisee. Now go up L(N) over an easy rounded ridge of snow and rock leading to the SW ridge. Do not take the couloir W or E of pt.2942m. (a distinct slabby area of rock seemingly joined to the SW ridge), steep and dangerous. Follow the easy rounded ridge and meet the SW ridge at any convenient spot; follow it easily to summit (4–5h.).

North-East Ridge (Hinter). *A fairly long and somewhat tedious route, but useful if a round traverse is contemplated from Gelmer to Grimsel via Gerstenhörner and Nägelisgrätli. No technical difficulties, but tricky route finding in bad weather.* I.

88. From the Gelmer hut follow Route 81 up to Bergli. Now cross SE and reach the edge of the Gelmer glacier immediately S of pt.2794m. Cross the glacier (a few crevasses), then climb mixed snow and rock without difficulty to saddle just N of the Hinter Gerstenhorn. From this saddle follow the ridge on somewhat loose blocks to summit (3–4h.).

West Flank. *A long strenuous approach over difficult and somewhat awkward terrain. Several routes have been done on these walls in this area, but not recorded. For those fit and interested enough it is an excellent training ground, with a good chance of doing a new route, especially on the Mittler Gerstenhorn.*

89. Leave the Grimsel road just S of the Gerstenbach (torrent); a little above the dam wall of the Räterichsbodensee. Climb steeply on rock and grass to pt.2852m., keeping L (N) of pt. 2621m. at foot of the Gerstenbach glacier. Cross the glacier (easy) to any saddle between any of the three summits as in Route 87 and reach the top along the ridges (4–5h.).

SCHAUBHORN   2683.6m.

A minor summit S of the Gelmersee, forming the end of the Hinter Gerstenhorn ridge. It is rarely climbed.
    Possibility of new face climbs on the S walls above Tälteni but can only be reached from pt.1858m. on the Gelmer hut path. Very long, difficult and strenuous merely to reach the wall.

NÄGELISGRÄTLI   2661m.

The shortest way from the Grimsel pass (2165m.) to Furka (2431m.) via the Belvédère Hotel. One of the finest walking tours in this part of the Alps, affording magnificent panoramic views. Used by Sir Martin Conway, July, 1894, in his ascent of the Galenstock. An old established route.

From Grimsel Pass.

90. From top of the Grimsel pass, go behind the small stone church and follow the path rising steeply past pt.2395m. Continue by pt.2481m. to the Schirm hut (not a mtn. hut); small lake down to L. Follow the path round behind the hut and up to a small lake—Grätlisee, pt.2661m. Shortly after this the path descends steeply in a series of zigzags to a small lake on the W side of the Rhone glacier, pt.2340m. Now cross the dry but crevassed glacier SE to pt.2380m. where the path along moraine to the Hotel Belvédère is joined (3–4h., somewhat shorter in reverse direction). N.B. The Hotel is still 157m. below top of the Furka pass.

The Nägelisgrätli can also be reached by a path which leaves the Grimsel road at pt.1923m. beside the Grimsel lake. This is longer and steeper, lacking the height advantage of the pass.

PART II

DAMMASTOCK GROUP

This central group, incorporating some of the highest mtns. in this part of Switzerland, consists of a high level ridge running from the Kl. Furkahorn above the Furka pass, more or less directly N to the Eggstock at the head of the Rhone glacier. The most important peaks are the Galenstock, Tiefenstock and Dammastock, the latter being the highest in the W Urner Alps.

Most of the climbing is of a serious nature, demanding experience in dealing with mixed terrain and complicated glaciers. Even the low graded routes should not be undertaken lightly owing to the remote nature of the peaks.

The most south-easterly arm running from the main ridge affords some splendid climbing for the rock specialist on the Kl. and Gr. Büelenhörner, with only minor glacier problems.

With the exception of the latter, the area is well served by the Damma and Kehlenalp huts. Although the Albert Heim hut can be used for the Büelenhorn, this peak is within easy reach of the Furka pass and there is plenty of scope for camping close to the walls. The Hotel Belvédère is a useful if somewhat expensive base for climbs on the Kl. and Gr. Furkahorn, Galengrat and Galenstock.

KLEIN FURKAHORN   3026.2m.

A small easy mtn.; a popular viewpoint above the Furka pass.
First ascent: Birchtold, 10 August, 1836.

South-West Ridge. *An easy much frequented route.* I. *Diagram, p.56.*

91. From Hotel Belvédère follow the ridge easily to summit (2½h. from hotel).

East Flank. *Another easy route, not popular.* I.

92. From Büelenstafel on the Furka pass follow the

53

Sidelenbach (stream) E, then go up the E ridge, over scree and large blocks to summit (2h. from Büelenstafel).

North Ridge. *The best and most difficult route on the mtn.* II. *First ascent: Th. Montigel, 1908. Diagram, p.56.*
93. From the S Galengratlücke (Routes 101/102) climb the ridge, keeping to the crest where possible, over a series of interesting rocky towers to the summit. The summit block is climbed by a gully on E (L) side (3½–4h. from Furka pass).

GALENGRAT   3049m., 3115m., 3169m. and 3217m.
A wild impressive rock ridge with numerous pts. and summits running from the Kl. Furkahorn to the Galensattel at the foot of the Galenstock S ridge. A good climb, but seldom done, is to traverse the complete ridge from S to N. III+. First traverse done piecemeal by Th. Montigel, 1 August and 30 September, 1909, and 2 October, 1910.

Pt.3049m.
A prominent rock tower, not usually climbed for its own sake but taken in or by-passed while climbing the Kl. Furkahorn N ridge (Route 93).

Pt.3115m. or **Sidelenhorn.**

S ridge. *Not a difficult route, interesting.* II. *Diagram, p.56.*
94. From the S Galengratlücke (Routes 101/102) follow the wide block-line ridge to S summit, then along the narrow serrated ridge, turning two fine rock towers on SW side (40–50 min. from the lücke).

Pt.3169m. or **Gross Furkahorn.**
A splendid mtn. The summit consists of several impressive rock pinnacles, affording interesting acrobatic climbing.

South Ridge. *A good climb; quite difficult.* III. *Diagram, p.56.*

95. From the S Galengratlücke climb the serrated ridge, keeping to the crest where possible or turning difficulties on the W (L) side as necessary. The first main tower is taken by an obvious chimney (2h. from lücke).

West Wall. *A short climb in magnificent surroundings.* II. *First ascent: J. A. Luttmann-Johnson with Peter Almer, 6 August 1896. Diagram, p.56.*

96. From Hotel Belvédère follow the E edge of the Rhone glacier N to pt.2391m. Bear R and follow the stream over grass and scree to foot of the wall. Climb this direct to summit (2½–3h. from hotel).

North Ridge. *Another short climb, interesting.* II. *Diagram, p.56.*

97. From the N Galengratlücke (Route 103) follow the ridge to summit, turning two difficult gendarmes on W (R) side (30 min. from lücke).

East Rib. *Quite a good climb; the best on E side.* II+, *or more difficult depending on variants taken. First ascent: Karl Baumann and Otto Coninx, 23 September, 1946.*

98. From Büelenstafel on the Furka pass follow the Sidelenbach stream to the snow, then slant up N over the Sidelen glacier to foot of the well-marked E rib. Go a little round to the N and get on to the rib beside a small shoulder. Climb the rib pleasantly to summit, turning difficulties as necessary to the N (R) (3–3½h. from Büelenstafel).

Pt.3217m. or Zeltspitz (Gross Sidelenhorn)

The highest summit in the Galengrat and the last pt. in the ridge before the Galensattel.

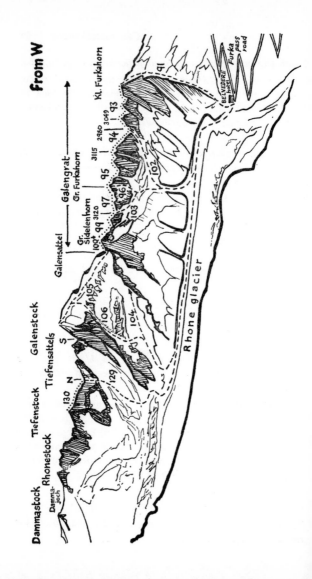

From W

Dammastock Tiefenstock Galenstock

Rhonestock Tiefensattels

Damma-joch

130 N S

129

106 104

105

Galensattel Galengrat

Gr. Sidelenhorn Gr. Furkahorn

3120 3115 3049 2980

100 99 97 96 95 94 93 91

98 102 103 Kl. Furkahorn

Rhone glacier

BELVEDERE hotel Furka pass road

South Ridge. *The most difficult and one of the best routes on the Galengrat.* III+. *First descended: W. Klinger and Th. Montigel, 1 August, 1909. First ascent: Karl Baumann and Otto Coninx, 3 August, 1947. Diagram, p.56.*

99. From the N Galengratlücke (Route 103) cross a tall impressive gendarme and reach the gap behind. Climb a gully to the E for 30m. to a terrace. Traverse up across a slab to a vague dièdre which cuts the steep slabby wall. Climb this for 30m. to a good stance, then slant R over easier rock to a somewhat grassy rib which is followed L on to the ridge. Follow the ridge pleasantly to below the summit block which is climbed by a difficult crack on SE side (1½h. from lücke).

From North-East. *The normal descent route. Easy.* I. *First ascent: O. Kielsberg and J. J. Schiesse with Zgraggen, 2 September, 1892. Diagram, p.56.*

100. From the Galensattel (Route 104) follow the easy ridge to summit (30 min. from sattel).

SOUTH GALENGRATLÜCKE   c.2980m.

Not marked on LK. The deepest gap between pt.3049m. and pt.3115m. Rarely used as a pass in the true sense but occasionally in conjunction with the Nägelisgrätli, with the object of making a direct cross-country route to the Albert Heim hut. First crossing: Gottlieb Studer and R. Kernen with Peter and Andreas Sulzer, 1 August, 1868.

From East. *Easy.*

101. From the small group of chalets just below top of the Furka pass (E) follow the path past pt.2514.2m. then up to pt.2689m. Go W steeply over snow and scree and finally up a snow or scree filled gully to pass (3h.).

From West. *Easy. Diagram, p.56.*

102. From Hotel Belvédère go N up the E side of the Rhone glacier to pt.2391m. Now bear R (E) over steep grass, scree and rocks to the pass (1½h.).

NORTH GALENGRATLÜCKE   c.3120m.

The deepest saddle in ridge between pts.3169m. and 3217m., unnamed on LK. It should not be regarded as a pass, only as a means of attaining the N section of the Galengrat. Only the W approach is described; that from the E is difficult and very unpleasant. First ascent: J. Kürsteiner with Franz Zgraggen, 6 September, 1906.

From West. *Diagram, p.56.*

103. From Hotel Belvédère follow Route 96 to below W wall of the Gr. Furkahorn. Go somewhat further N over snow, then climb a short steep couloir to the lücke ($1\frac{1}{2}$–2h. from hotel).

GALENSATTEL   3113m.

A small saddle between pt.3217m. on the Galengrat and the Galenstock. Only the ascent from W is recommended; that from E can be very icy, difficult and dangerous from stonefall. Its main use is as a descent route from pt.3217m. and as a means of access to the Galenstock S ridge. First ascent (from E): W. Klingler and Th. Montigel, 1 August, 1909.

From West. *Easy.*

104. From Hotel Belvédère follow Route 96 on the Rhone glacier, up past pt.2391m. till level with a small glacier cwm up to the R. This is below pt.2769m. Ascend this small unnamed glacier on its R (S) side, avoiding the small icefall; then climb ENE, finally over scree or snow to saddle ($3\frac{1}{2}$h. from hotel). *Diagram, p.56.*

GALENSTOCK   3583.1m.

One of the finest and most impressive mtns. in this part of the Swiss Alps. An isolated peak, it holds a commanding position over all the surrounding mtns. and ridges. All the routes are of a serious nature, demanding a knowledge of combination climbing on rock, snow and ice. The cornices can sometimes be very dangerous and special attention should be paid to these.

South Ridge (Galengrat). *An interesting climb on a fine snow ridge. I/II., depending on conditions. First ascent: E. Desor, D. Dollfuss–Ausset and Daniel Dollfuss with Hans Wähun, Hans Jaun, Melchior Bannholzer and D. Brigger, 18 August, 1845. Diagrams, p.56, 63, 72.*

105. From Hotel Belvédère follow Route 104 to just below the Galensattel. Now slant up L across the SW flank and join the ridge above; or climb the ridge directly from the sattel. Follow the snow ridge to summit; the final slope is fairly steep and sometimes icy. Keep to the W side as much as possible to avoid the cornice to the E (2–2½h. from the Galensattel).

South-West Rib. *A good mixed route, somewhat more difficult than 105. II. First descent: Louis and Marcel Kurz with Sebastian Hischier, 17 July, 1901. Diagram, p.56.*

106. Follow Route 104 to the middle of the small glacier just below the Galensattel. Traverse round to the NW, to join the rib at pt.3008m. This traverse can be icy (crampons useful). Climb the rib on good rock, turning difficulties as necessary to L (N), up to the final steep summit snow slope which is followed to top (3½–4h. from Rhone glacier).

North Ridge. *The normal route, a popular climb from the Albert Heim hut. No difficulties in good conditions, but care should be taken in descent, especially in bad weather, not to descend too far S over the Tiefen glacier; bad crevasses and quite dangerous. It is always best to keep bearing round N, towards the Tiefenstock–Gletschhorn cwm, to avoid crevasses. I/II, depending on conditions. First ascent: Charles and Paul Montandon, 1 July, 1902. Diagram, p.60.*

107. Descend W from the Albert Heim hut and follow the made-path across scree WNW to above pt.2713m. Ascend the Tiefen glacier in the same direction (WNW) to below the S. Tiefensattel; this lies immediately N of pt.3438m. (Route 127). Work S and slightly downwards below the ridge to reach a distinct terrace which runs up to a depression in the ridge

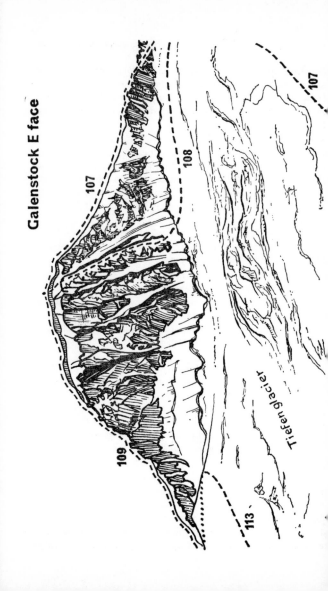

Galenstock E face

107

108

107

109

113

Tiefenglacier

about 50m. from where the snow ridge starts. Climb the spiky ridge, keeping to the W (R) side, then along the summit ridge, a mixture of snow and rock to top. The ridge can also be followed in its entirety from the S. Tiefensattel; this is more difficult and longer (5h. from Albert Heim hut).

East Wall. *Three well-defined rock ribs run up this wall; the most northerly leads direct to summit and is the recommended line of ascent. Not a difficult climb, interesting and worthwhile. I/II. First ascent: W. E. Burger and H. Lauper, 26 June, 1921. Diagram, p.60.*

108. From the Albert Heim hut follow Route 107, down below the E wall. Cross the bergschrund and reach the first rocks of the rib. Climb this easily and pleasantly to a short snow ridge leading direct to summit. Huge cornice possible. (3½–4h. from hut).

South-East Ridge. *A fine climb on an impressive ridge. III. First ascent: Rudolf Martin with Josef Püntener, 7 September, 1902. Second ascent: J. J. Withers, 5 September, 1903. Diagrams, p.60, 63, 72.*

109. From the Obere Büelenlücke (Route 113) climb a small secondary ridge of rock or snow, then R (N) over the Tiefen glacier to the bergschrund. Cross this, sometimes difficult, and get on to rocks of the true SE ridge. Avoid the first great tower by a chimney couloir to the N (R). It is not recommended to climb it direct. Now follow the crest of the ridge, turning the towers when necessary either N or S according to difficulty, to reach the S ridge about 15 min. below summit (2–3h. from lücke, 4–5h., from Albert Heim hut).

South-East Rib and South-East Wall. *An excellent climb, not as popular as it deserves, as it necessitates starting from the road. If a hut is ever built in the Galenstock–Büelenhorn cirque a considerable amount of climbing would be done from this side. Pts.2882m. and 3253m. offer splendid opportunities for short* *severe routes on good rock, as well as the numerous climbs on the Büelenhorn.* III. *First ascent: R. v. Wyss and M. v. Wyss, 29 September, 1901. Diagram, p.72.*

110. From Büelenstafel on the Furka pass climb N towards the Büelenhorn, following a faint track. Bear NW some distance below this mtn. and cross scree to reach the Sidelen glacier. Practically any route can be taken to reach this pt (see Route 111). Ascend this easy glacier to the great rock towers of pt.2882m. (no crevasses) in the middle. Pass these to the W (L) then up E (R) to reach a secondary snow ridge leading up from this pt. Follow the ridge to a connecting rock rib on the main mtn. and climb a steep 5m. wall direct to reach easier rocks above. Turn and avoid a large reddish buttress on its S (L) side, then climb fairly steep and exposed rock directly to the S ridge above, which is followed to summit (4½–5h. from Büelenstafel).

South Wall (to pt.3252m.). *A splendid free climb on excellent rock and to-date the most difficult on the mtn. Several run-outs are long and a good selection of pegs and wedges should be taken. 300m., V with pitches of V+ and VI−. First ascent: Dieter Kienast and Hans-Peter Geier, 6 August, 1967. Diagram, p.72.*

111. From the small group of chalets, 2427m. just below (E) the top of the Furkapass follow a small track up to the Sidelen glacier. Slant up NW below pt.2882m. to reach the foot of the wall which forms a small cwm (1½h. from road).

The climb starts below a slabby dièdre on the R-hand side of the wall and follows the line of a distinct red dièdre in the upper section. Climb on good holds for 10m. to the foot of the slabby dièdre, then up L by an adjoining crack (2 pegs) to slabs which are climbed for about 40m. to the L (5 pegs). Directly up at first, then R up to a crack (2 pegs) which leads up R to a distinct dièdre (5 pegs). A few m. up this, then it is possible to traverse R to a stance on the edge (1 peg); good belay but a small stance (45m.). Climb the crack system above (R) for 25m (4 pegs) to a ramp which slants R to a good stance. In the same

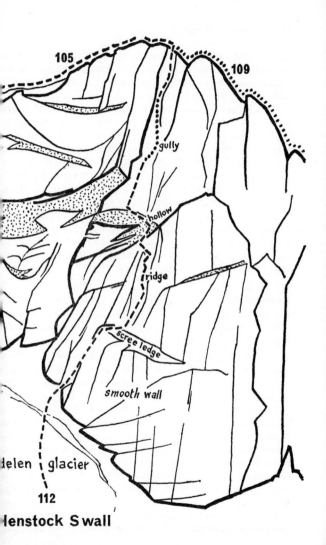

105
109
gully
hollow
ridge
scree ledge
smooth wall
delen glacier
112
lenstock S wall

direction take a crack, then up L on good holds to a corner crack (1 peg). Climb this to the top (2 pegs) then across the L-hand wall to a good stance; 40m. pitch. Continue L up slabby rocks for 40m. (1 peg) to a terrace.

From here a further 40m. on steep rock with good holds leads towards the large red dièdre. A short steep crack leads to this (1 peg). Climb the dièdre for 40m. to a good stance. Now take a steep crack at the back of the dièdre (1 peg), then move out to the L edge. Cross this for a few m., a short traverse L., then back R up slabby rock (2 pegs) for 40m. to a large stance in the back of the dièdre. Climb L past a large jammed block, using a crack (1 peg), which leads back R into the dièdre. Continue in the dièdre to a good stance; 45m. pitch (2 pegs, 2 wedges). Continue a further 40m. up the steep dièdre, turning another jammed block, and in 15m. or so reach the top. The main summit can be reached in about 30 min. from this pt. along the S ridge (Route 105) (8–10h.).

South Wall. *A splendid new route on this 400m. wall.* V+; *the last 100m. to the top are over snow and ice. First ascent: Max Niedermann and Ernst Renner, 16 July, 1967. Diagrams, p.63, 72.*

112. Ascend the Sidelen glacier NW (Routes 111/123) to its upper end below the face, and start high up on L, above a large, smooth glaciated wall. Cross a large schrund, climb R to a chimney and up this 40m. (1 peg) to a small scree ledge on R. Cross this, 8–10m. R., then climb direct for three rope-lengths over slabs to a ridge. Follow this to its top to reach a large hollow, easily seen from below. At its highest pt. follow a ledge L for 10–15m. to below a steep, slabby, bulging wall. Climb this for two rope-lengths (4–5 pegs) to a gully. Climb this R for a rope-length to reach a corner crack. Climb its L side (3–4 pegs, 1 wedge) and reach a platform; stance. A further rope-length over blocky rock leads to below an overhang; belay peg.

Traverse R below the overhang to a crack and up this (pegs, wedges) to a cracked slab; stance. Go 3–4m. R, then up a 15m

labby wall to below very steep rocks; stance. Now climb the
wall above for 2–3 rope-lengths to the summit ridge, which is
climbed over snow/ice to top (10h. on first ascent).

OBERE BÜELENLÜCKE   3225m.

Not marked on LK.1:50,000 but is named with its height on the
new LK.1:25,000. It lies at the foot of the Galenstock SE ridge
NW of pt.3253m. Serves as a means of access to the Galenstock SE ridge. Usually it is approached from the Albert Heim
hut, this side being far more convenient and easier than that
from the Furka, which is longer and can be far more difficult
and complicated.

From East. *Easy. Diagram, p.60.*

113. From the Albert Heim hut go W on to the Tiefen glacier
and make for the prominent rocky rib, pt.2906 (LK.1:25,000)
which lies parallel with the N face of the Gross Büelenhorn,
3206.8m. Keep S of this rib over easy uncrevassed névé to reach
the lücke (2–2½h. from hut).

This pt. can also be reached by following Route 108 and
continuing down below the E side of the Galenstock.

From South-West. *Usually fairly easy but there can be complications with crevasses and the bergschrund. First ascent of this
side: Rudolf Martin with G. Püntener, 7 September, 1902.
Diagram, p.72.*

114. From the Furka pass follow Routes 110/124 up to the
Sidelen glacier. Go up the middle of this glacier E (R) of pt.
2887m., then bear more R (E) towards the rocks of the Gr.
Büelenhorn SW walls. Skirt below these rocks till below the
lücke, then climb the most northerly of two snow couloirs to
the top. The bergschrund at the foot of this couloir can be very
difficult and there are usually large crevasses just before this
pt. (3–3½h. from pass).

GROSS BÜELENHORN   3206.8m.

An impressive twin headed granite peak rising E from the Sidelen glacier. Two extremely difficult routes have been made on the S wall, but undoubtedly the finest line is the W pillar. A good classic climb is to traverse the E and NW summits from the Unter Büelenlücke to the Obere Büelenlücke. Until recently the mtn. was relatively unknown, but is now becoming increasingly popular. For the longer more difficult climbs it is recommended to bivouac just below the Sidelen glacier; there is plenty of water and numerous suitable boulders. This is only applicable for those coming from the Furka pass; the best and most convenient approach for the W wall routes is from the Albert Heim hut over the Untere Büelenlücke (Route 123). First ascent: R. Helbling, H. Biehly and V. de Beauclair, 24 August, 1902.

North Face and East Ridge. *A good climb within easy access of the Albert Heim hut. III. If the crest of the E ridge is followed (far more interesting and recommended) the route definitely becomes both harder and longer. IV. First ascensionists. First ascent of true E ridge: J. Marmet and G. Styger, 6 June, 1949.*

115. From the Albert Heim hut follow Route 112 to below the N face of the mtn. An obvious snow couloir runs up to the deep gap between the E and NW summits. Climb the E (L) side, then trend L on the N face to just below an obvious and distinct gap in the E ridge (this is the point where the ridge can be climbed in its entirety). Now bear R, keeping below the ridge, and so reach the summit ($3\frac{1}{2}$–4h. from the hut).

North Couloir and North-West Ridge. *Not a climb of great merit but it serves as a useful descent route. III. Descended by first ascensionists.*

116. Follow the snow couloir of Route 115 directly to gap between the two summits. Climb a difficult chimney SW of the ridge crest then a series of blocks to summit ($2\frac{1}{2}$–3h.).

South-East Flank. *A short, fairly interesting climb. III.*

117. From the Untere Büelenlücke (Route 123) start somewhat R (E) of the S ridge. Climb a crack, then ledges and short walls.

Finally a series of grooves and gullies lead to E summit. Avoid the buttress-like barrier on the upper part of the S ridge by traversing E (1½h. from the lücke).

South Ridge. *A very good climb; the classic way of traversing the mtn., taking in the NW summit then descending to the Obere Büelenlücke. IV with one pitch of V. First ascent and traverse of mtn: A. and O. Amstad with Guido Masetto, 19 August, 1935. Diagram, p.73.*

118. From the Untere Büelenlücke (Route 123) climb easily over blocks and short rocky steps to the first barrier. Go R from its edge and climb an open dièdre for 20m. to a small bulge. Traverse R over easy rocks, then return to the ridge below the second barrier. Climb the first few m. on the edge, then trend L with difficulty. Now climb pleasantly and more easily, keeping to the ridge crest, to a narrow horizontal section. This part is cut by a deep cleft which must be jumped. Follow the ridge to a gap below a smooth, yellow rock tower. Avoid this on the W side, then regain the ridge by slanting up R. Finally follow the ridge pleasantly to the E summit (3–4h. from lücke).

North-West Summit and descent by NW ridge. III. *First ascended in conjunction with S ridge (Route 118). Diagram, p.73.*

119. From the E summit descend Route 116 to gap between the two summits. Climb the ridge on a good rock to the NW summit, keeping to its R side. From the top descend the crenellated NW ridge to the Obere Büelenlücke, turning a large tower on its R side. (Several alternatives are available for reaching gap from the NW summit, either by climbing down or abseiling). A long rope for abseiling is useful. This can be very complicated and difficult in bad weather (2–3h. from E summit).

South-West Wall (Baumann–Müller Route). *An excellent climb, difficult and sustained on perfect rock. A good selection of pegs and wedges should be taken. VI, A3, 450m. First ascent: Baumann and Müller, 1961.*

When viewed from the Sidelen glacier a pale flame-like pillar marks the W side of the NW summit block. The L-hand edge of this pillar running down to the glacier forms the W pillar route (*Route 121*). To the R the smooth upper part of the SW wall drops to a large recess behind a secondary triangular pillar, the top of which is approx. in line with the E summit. This pillar is cut to the L and R by two distinct faults which lead down to the glacier. Both routes on the SW wall start at these two respective lines. Diagram, p.73.

120. From the Furka pass follow Route 111 on to the Sidelen glacier (2½h.), or from the Albert Heim hut (Route 123) (2h.). Start at the L fault of the triangular pillar. This fault which takes the form of an overhanging dièdre lies to the R of a line descending from the upper flame-like pillar. Climb this dièdre for three rope-lengths; 110m., A2, A3, pegs and wedges. Now climb slabby rocks for about two rope-lengths to foot of the upper wall. Climb a crack then overhanging rocks above by an overhanging corner crack (V/VI, A2). Continue in this to below an overhang, then traverse 6m. R to a slabby section. Take a crack on the L leading back to the dièdre (V/VI), then go L to a ledge. A further 8m. L to a crack; climb this to a small ledge. Traverse L to a slab and climb this to below an overhang. Climb this both free and artificial (VI, A2), then trend a few m. R and follow a crack which leads on the L side of the summit pillar to top (16h. for first ascent, bivouac).

South-West Wall (Niedermann-Anderrüthi Route). *The original route on the wall, of comparable standard and quality with the Baumann–Müller climb, but with more free climbing and less artificial. The start is not so direct and is less attractive. VI, A2, 450m. First ascent: Max Niedermann and F. Anderrüthi, 1956. Diagram, p.73.*

121. The climb starts approx. 100m. SE of Route 120 and takes the R fault of the triangular pillar. Climb the L-hand side of the deep gully for about three rope-lengths (V). At the top slant R

over easy slabby rock to top of the pillar. Now follow an obvious
ledge L to a dièdre coming in a line through the upper wall
from the summit. Climb this for three rope-lengths to a niche
below a projecting block (VI, A2). From here climb a further
10m. direct to below an overhang, which is climbed on its L side;
continue for 5m. to a ring peg. Pendule down L for 10m. to a
small stance then climb L to a detached block (V+, VI). Now
climb L for 5m. in a steep crack, then up R for 4m. to below an
overhang which is turned on its R side (VI, wedges). A steep,
narrow dièdre now leads to another overhang which is climbed
direct, thence the summit (12h. for first ascent).

West Pillar. *This route follows the sharp W edge of the prominent
summit pillar (see preamble, Route 120) and is undoubtedly the
finest climb and best line on the mtn. Free climbing on excellent
granite with only one section of artificial. V+, A3, 400m. Pegs
and wedges (2–4cm.) should be taken. First ascent: Fritz Villiger
and Kurt Grüter, 15/16 August, 1964. Diagram, p.73.*

122. The climb starts about 200m. NW from Route 120 at the
foot of a distinct couloir marking the L side of the pillar. Ascend
névé in the lower part of the gully; cross a schrund, then go R
and get on to the rocks. Climb the pillar for a short distance,
then go L for a few m. in the gully till it is practicable to return R
to the pillar and reach a small ledge. From here climb on good
holds to the foot of a series of steep cracks. Follow these, then
climb delicately to below an overhang. Make a rising traverse L
to the pillar edge, then climb an overhanging chimney/crack
(key pitch, A3). Continue up the steep exposed edge to a large
stance. Climb a slab L to a dièdre and follow this to a huge
split slab. The next dièdre leads to a small terrace below a
delicate slab. Climb this slab, then a series of short, steep
walls to the upper pillar ridge. Climb this more or less direct to
the summit block which is turned to the L on the NW side
(11h. for first ascent).

UNTERE BÜELENLÜCKE   c.2900m.

An easy snow pass between the Gr. and Kl. Büelenhorn. A convenient means of access to climbs on the former mtn. from the Albert Heim hut. The pass is marked by two rock towers, dolomitic in appearance, with several lesser towers and accompanying buttresses. Both these spires afford interesting though short climbs.

From West.

123. From the Albert Heim hut follow Route 113 over the Tiefen glacier to beneath the lower rocks of the Gr. Büelenhorn E ridge. Now work SW over easy névé (no crevasses) and reach the pass immediately N of the N tower (1¼h. from hut).

From South-East. *Diagram, p.73.*

124. From the Furka pass follow Route 111 to the Sidelen glacier. Practically any route can be taken from the road. From the little lake just below the glacier and N of pt.2623m., bear R (NE) past pt.2727m. and finally in the same direction over scree and snow to the pass, N of the towers (1½–2h. from road).

KLEIN BÜELENHORN

A minor mtn., but with a splendid S wall, seen to advantage on E side of the Furka pass. It is rarely climbed from any other side.

South Wall. *An excellent climb, steep, difficult and exposed on good rock. VI, A2, 350m. The wall is easily reached N from Büelenstafel, pt.2254m. on the Furka pass, in 1½h. First ascent: Martial Perrenoud and Willy Mottet, 30 June, 1957 in 7h. First British ascent: J. O. Talbot and Martin Epp, 1963. Diagrams, p.71, 73.*

125. The climb starts in a direct line with the summit. Well to the R of this line is a large terrace topped by a series of over-hangs. Climb a large open chimney for at least 30m. (IV), then

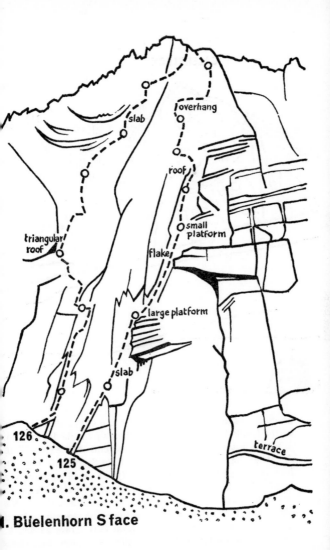

overhang

slab

roof

small platform

triangular roof

flake

large platform

slab

126

125

terrace

Büelenhorn S face

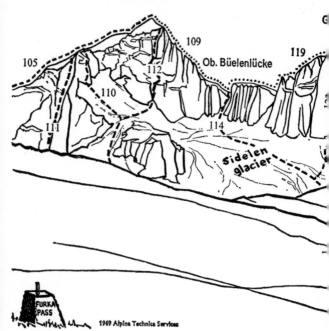

GALENSTOCK

105   109   119   Ob. Büelenlücke

110   112   111   114

Sidelen glacier

FURKA PASS

1969 Alpina Technica Services

go up the next dièdre for 80m. (IV+) to a split slab. Take this
on the L side (A2, pegs), then continue up the dièdre for 20m.
to where it is possible to get on to a good stance (V). Climb
direct for 5m., then continue up a flake that slants L (V+),
followed by a short delicate pitch (V) to a small platform in a
small dièdre L; good stance. Follow this dièdre and a series
of cracked, broken blocks to below a small roof. Climb this
(A2, pegs), then exit free along the top of the sloping roof and
up a small dièdre to a stance above (VI). Traverse 5m. L,
climb steeply for 10m. (IV+), then climb a smooth steep ramp

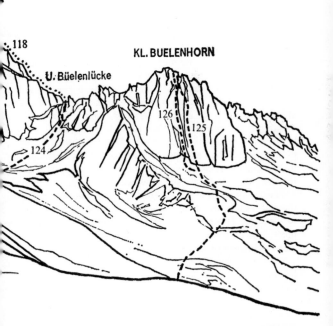

SIDELEN GLACIER BASIN from S

118

KL. BUELENHORN

U. Büelenlücke

126
125

124

L to reach the foot of a large dièdre (V+); poor stance. Go up this dièdre for 10m. (V), then turn an overhang on the R (4 pegs, A2). Return to the dièdre and climb it to the top; reach a large terrace. Difficulties relent and several easy ways can be found to the summit ridge. The summit itself can be reached more or less direct by an obvious chimney ($4\frac{1}{2}$–6h. from foot).

South-South-West Wall. *A good interesting climb on excellent rock, though not as difficult as the Perrenoud–Mottet route. It follows a line more or less direct to the summit. Near the top are* *two distinct U-shaped grassy terraces; the climb passes R of these and finishes on the E summit ridge close to Route 125. These two climbs are parallel and quite close together, but are separated in the lower half by a slabby buttress. V, 350m. First ascent: Robi Hugentobler, Dieter Kienast, Heinz and Margrit Bächli, 27 July, 1966. Diagrams, p.71, 73.*

126. An obvious double dièdre about 50m. above the foot of the wall marks the first feature of the climb. Start 20m. L of this line, then slant R to below it. Climb the dièdre, starting at the L side, and finishing to the R. At the top traverse L for 5m. to a stance. Go up L for a short distance, then follow a dièdre slanting R for at least 8m. Now climb L for 30m. to a stance below a yellow, three-cornered roof. Trend slightly R for 30m., then traverse R into a dièdre which runs L at first then directly up to a gap between a tower and the wall; stance. Climb direct for 30m., then make a rising traverse R for 10m. to a stance. This is now exactly level with the first grassy terrace L. Climb the slab above, trend R for about 20m., then climb slightly L to a stance. This is above the second grassy terrace L. Now finally make a slightly rising traverse R to the E summit ridge close to the exit of Route 125 (4–5h. from foot).

The way off is an easy scramble along the NE flank near the NE ridge, down to its lowest gap, then descend either N to the Albert Heim or S to the Furka pass road.

SOUTH AND NORTH TIEFENSATTELS

Two easy passes, the former situated at foot of the Galenstock N ridge, the latter below the Tiefenstock S ridge. Only the N sattel is used as a pass connecting the Tiefen and Rhone glaciers, the S is merely used for access to the Galenstock. The ridge between the two sattels can be traversed easily and pleasantly on good rock in about 2h.

South Tiefensattel. *From the East—easy but care should be taken not to go too far S into a zone of bad crevasses.*

127. From the Albert Heim hut go W to above pt.2713m. and reach the Tiefen glacier. Ascend this glacier WNW, avoiding the crevasses L, to below the sattel, easily recognised as a deep gap in the ridge. Climb the snow/scree gully directly to top. Sometimes late in the season there can be a bergschrund, and at any time a cornice on top (2–2½h. from hut).

North Tiefensattel (3335.4m.). *From the East—Easy, similar to Route 127. First crossing: Rudolf and W. Lindt with Peter and Andreas Sulzer, 14 September, 1867.*

128. From the Albert Heim hut climb NW from the Tiefen glacier to below the pass which is easily recognised. Climb a snow gully, sometimes quite rocky, easily to top (2½h. from hut).

From the West—Easy; nevertheless a far more serious glacier proposition, requiring a fair degree of experience. It would hardly seem justifiable from the Hotel Belvédère, but more useful in conjunction with the Nägelisgrätli (Route 90), or the Obere Triftlimmi (Route 83). Map and compass essential. Diagram, p.56.

129. From E side of the Rhone glacier, in a direct line E of the Tällistock, 3185m. and N of pt.3022m., climb E over fairly steep and crevassed glacier to a rock band. Ascend these rocks, then climb a short but easy snow ice couloir to top (1½–2 hr. from 2900m. contour on glacier).

TIEFENSTOCK   3515.4m.

A fine rock peak dominating the head of the Tiefen glacier (NW), with a number of first class routes, all in easy reach of the Albert Heim hut over an uncomplicated glacier. It was first ascended by the W flank and S ridge from the Rhone glacier; this easy route is now rarely done, being too long an approach for a climb of so little merit. Any climber so wishing to do it can use his own route finding ability. First ascent: M. Rosenmund with F. Kreuzer and L. zum Oberhaus, 22 July, 1882.

South Ridge. *An easy climb, the normal route for ascent or descent to or from the Albert Heim hut. I. First ascent: A. Lom* *with Jos. Gentinetta, 25 September, 1885. Diagram, p.56.*

130. From the Albert Heim hut follow Route 127 across the Tiefen glacier to the N Tiefensattel. Now climb the S ridge over easy blocks and snow to summit (3–3½h. from hut).

South Rib and South-East Ridge. *An excellent climb on good rock and not too difficult. The route follows the well-marked rocky rib which descends from pt.3359m. into the upper NW Tiefen glacier cwm. IV−. First ascent: Helene Kuntze with Joseph and Gabriel Lochmatter, 23 July, 1903. First descended: C. Seelig with J. Mattli, 18 August, 1890.*

131. From the Albert Heim hut follow Route 127 on to the Tiefen glacier. Ascend the glacier directly NW to the rib forming the R-hand arm of the cwm. Climb an easy scree gully W of the rib to reach its crest which is followed on good rock to the SE ridge just above pt.3359m. Now climb the ridge traversing the towers to summit. The first tower can be avoided by a ledge on the N (R) side, but this is not so pleasant or enjoyable even though easier (5–6h. from hut).

North-East Ridge. *A good interesting combination climb of rock and glacier work. The crevasses can sometimes be quite awkward. III. First ascent: C. Seelig with J. Mattli, 17 August 1890. Diagram, p.88.*

132. Follow Route 152 from the Damma hut as for the Damma pass, or Route 280 for the Ober Gletschjoch, to reach the upper Damma glacier. The latter is best, being the shortest and safest crossing in regard to the direction of the crevasses, and not in the same line as them as in the Damma pass route. The climb starts at the foot (pt.3132m.) of the rib which protrudes into the glacier from the SE ridge. Cross a bergschrund and turn the first barrier to the N, usually ice, then follow the ridge keeping to the crest as much as possible up to the SE ridge to join Route 131. Difficulties can be avoided on the E side, but the rock is poor; not recommended (6½–7h. from hut).

North Face. *Precious little is known of this route and only a brief indication can be given. A 400m. steep ice wall which should only be attempted early in the season when there is an abundance of hard packed frozen snow. Later on the face usually deteriorates in quality. IV, though sometimes easier or harder according to conditions. First ascent: S. Plietz and M. Bachmann, 9 June, 1935. Diagram, p.88.*

133. From the Damma hut follow Route 152 to the upper Damma glacier. Go further W past pt.3132m. to foot of the wall. Climb this directly as possible, finishing in a steep narrow snow ice couloir to reach a gap in the rocky summit ridge (6–7h. from hut).

North Ridge (from Unter Winterjoch). *Col, c.3450m. Neither the N ridge nor the Unter Winterjoch are recommended. The ridge is easy but uninteresting; access to the col is not easy and is subject to ice and stonefall. First ascent of Unter Winterjoch from Damma glacier: A. W. Moore and H. Walker with J. Anderegg and H. Bauman, 27 June, 1870. First ascent of N ridge: R. Helbling, H. Biehly and Alb. Weber, 8 August, 1901. Diagram, p.88.*

134. From the Damma glacier take either of two steep snow ice couloirs to the joch (approach from Damma hut, 5–6h.).

South Wall. *A splendid route on good rock; one of the best climbs on the mtn. V+, 350m. First ascent: Max Niedermann and Axel Pauls, 23 June, 1966. The mtn. has two summits; the route follows the E (R) pillar-like buttress which falls from the E summit. The pillar is divided into two distinct sections, the lowest being cut by an obvious dièdre. The route follows this line and is reached by a small rib which protrudes into the glacier. Diagram, p.78.*

135. From the Albert Heim hut follow Route 127 up past the S rib to below the wall. Climb the short initial rib for 15–20m. to foot of the dièdre and follow this (2–3 pegs). Now climb the L side of an open dièdre by a series of cracks and slabs for 3 rope-lengths (10 pegs) to below a roof; étrier stance. Climb this on the L and reach a 30m. smooth dièdre which is climbed

initial rib

135 *Tiefen glacier*

Tiefenstock S wall

with the aid of pegs. At the top traverse off L to a stance. Climb direct over a series of steps to a ledge on L side of a large dièdre. Traverse this ledge L to the middle of the flank, then go straight up a 15m. wall to a stance. Now ascend slabs and cracks (pegs and wedges), then traverse 30m. L to a large stance on the extreme L edge of the dièdre. Climb this L pillar-like edge till it merges into the upper wall; then climb a steep 25m. wall which ends in a large hollow. Trend R over rocky terrain inside the hollow to the summit wall. About 10m. L of the pillar edge climb an overhang (1 peg), then a further 10–12m. up to a stance. The last rope-length up a series of steep slabs (3 pegs) leads to summit (9h. from foot of wall on first ascent; allow 2–2½h. from hut).

DAMMAZWILLINGE   E c.3280m.   W c.3275m.

Two fine rock peaks, separated by the Zwillingsscharte, lying SE of the Tiefenstock and immediately NW of the Ober Gletschjoch. Although relatively small and unnamed by LK, the splendid walls and ridges afford some excellent climbing of a high standard. Two extreme climbs are the S wall and S pillar of the W summit and the classic is the traverse of the twin summits from W to E. The best climbs are from the Tiefen glacier, nearly all within easy access of the Albert Heim hut. The Zwillingsscharte is easily reached from the Tiefenglacier by a snow couloir (1h.).

East Summit (from Ober Gletschjoch). *A good short interesting route.* IV+; *if the direct variation is taken,* V. *First ascent: Helene Kuntze with Joseph and Gabriel Lochmatter, 23 July, 1903.*

136. From the Ober Gletschjoch (Route 279) climb a steep crack (a few m. N of the joch) for half a rope-length to a good stance. Exit R from the crack with the direct aid of pegs, then go up easier rocks by a series of cracks, ledges and short walls to a large slab. Climb this direct to the summit; or do not exit from the crack but climb it direct. Very difficult, the first 10m. being smooth and slightly overhanging. Now continue directly for at least two rope-lengths up steep cracks and then finally over progressively easier rocks to top (2–3h. for either route from joch).

East Summit (South Rib from Tiefen glacier). *Another short climb, but not as good or as difficult as Route 136.* III. *First ascent: R. Martin with G. Püntener, 4 September, 1904.*

137. Go up for one rope-length in the snow couloir of the Zwillingsscharte. Climb rocks E (R) of the couloir to join the S rib, which is followed pleasantly to summit (1½–2h. from glacier).

East Summit (from Zwillingsscharte). *An easy scramble of no merit, only referred to for descent or traversing.* I.

138. From the scharte climb easy broken rocks to summit (10–15 min.).

East Summit (East Ridge). *A recent interesting climb, but the start somewhat spoils it. About 250m., III/IV with two rope-lengths of V. First ascent: Edi Andres and Franz Anderrüthi, 25 June, 1967.*

139. From the Albert Heim hut follow Route 279 to the Ober Gletschjoch. Descend the gully on E side towards the Damma glacier till about 10m. above the bergschrund. This pt. can also be reached from the Damma hut. Go up rocky steps and easy slabs to a steep ridge; small stance with ring peg. From here move 2m. R in a small groove, then climb a dièdre for 40m. (6 pegs) to a small stance (1 peg). Now climb direct for about five rope-lengths, keeping to the ridge as much as possible, up a series of blocks and small cracks to below the summit block. Go up L to below a steep slab, then from a stance go R across slabs (3 pegs) to the ridge edge. Climb steeply and direct, finally on the narrow ridge to summit (3–4h. from start).

Descent to Ober Gletschjoch. *This is best taken as directly as possible by a series of abseils. A good long rope and a spare are useful.*

West Summit (North-East Ridge from Zwillingsscharte). *A pleasant climb; a pity there is not more of it.* III.

140. From the scharte cross a few m. W to foot of an obvious chimney. Climb this, somewhat loose, to the NE ridge at a pt. directly above the scharte. Now climb the ridge pleasantly to the last obstacle. Turn this easily on the N side by a ledge; finally climb a steep chimney to summit ($\frac{3}{4}$–1h. from scharte).

West Summit (South Pillar). *An excellent hard free climb, steep and exposed.* 250m. V *with pitches of* V+ *and one of* VI. *First ascent: Peter Arigoni and Hans-Peter Geier, 27 October, 1963. First British ascent: J. O. Talbot and Martin Epp, 1964. Diagram, p.82.*

141. From the Albert Heim hut follow Route 279 as for the Ober Gletschjoch. Go a further 200m. NW from the couloir descending from the joch, to the foot of the distinct reddish-yellow pillar. Climb up R across a slab (2 pegs) to a crack which is followed for 40m. (pegs) to a stance. Climb the crack on the R to its top (pegs), then up L to the foot of a smooth slab. Cross this L (pegs) to a very small stance, then go up L by cracks and slabs for 30m. (pegs, wedges) to a good stance. Now climb with considerable difficulty a 5m. smooth holdless slab, then over easier rocks for 25m. (2 pegs) to a stance. Move R and go up a chimney (2 pegs) for 30m. to a stance. Now L at first, then climb R (2 pegs) to a good stance on the pillar edge. Traverse R on good holds, then climb for 40m. in a chimney-like dièdre (pegs) to a stance. Continue up the dièdre for 15m. (4 pegs), then exit R and climb slabs for 10m. (wedges) to a stance. Go back L into the dièdre and climb it for 35m. (pegs, wedges) to reach a good stance on a scree terrace. Finally climb slabby rock for about 30m. to summit (6–8h. from foot; 1$\frac{1}{2}$–2h. to start from hut).

West Summit (South Wall). *Another first-class route on perfect rock.* 250m., IV/V+. *First ascent: Edi Andres and Franz Anderrüthi, 1 July, 1967. Diagram, p.82.*

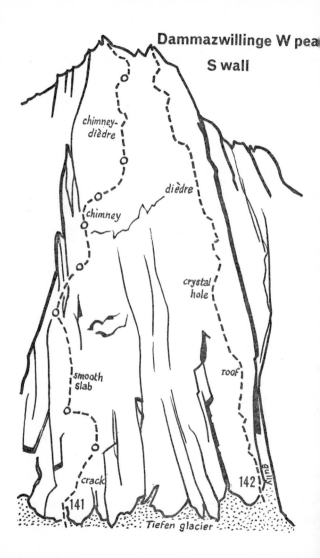

Dammazwillinge W peak
S wall

chimney-dièdre

dièdre

chimney

crystal hole

roof

smooth slab

crack

141

142

gully

Tiefen glacier

42. The climb starts 25m. R of the S pillar (Route 141), and about 5m. L of a distinct gully which cuts the R-hand side of the S wall. Climb a steep slab (1 peg) to a corner (2 pegs), then move R to a sort of pillar. Climb slabs (5 pegs), then slant R and climb a groove (1 peg) to a stance (2 pegs). Go directly up to a peg, then R and over slabs (6 pegs) to below a roof. Climb this on the L, then directly up with difficulty (5 pegs) to a stance (2 pegs). Climb L in a dièdre (1 peg), then R to a crystal hole with four distinct rocky heads. From the second head climb direct for 6m. (1 peg) to a small niche; stance (1 peg). Take a crack (2 pegs), traverse R then climb steeply to a break (6 pegs). Now go up a slab (1 peg) to a good stance (2 pegs). Climb a crack to the R (2 pegs), then slabs in a dièdre (3 pegs) to a tiny stance (2 pegs). Continue up the dièdre (3 pegs), then go L to a stance (1 peg). Now climb steeply to the pillar head (R) and continue up the next ridge to a terrace with 2 pegs to the R. Climb direct to a break, then take the L branch of a V-shaped crack to summit (6–8h. from the foot, which is reached in $1\frac{1}{2}$–2h. from hut).

West Summit (North-East Ridge). *The only route from the Damma hut, but a fine one taking a good line and well worth doing. The distinct ridge descends from the W summit to pt.2916m. on the Damma glacier. IV. First ascent: Marcel Kurz and Anton Simmen, 15 July, 1918.*

143. From the Damma hut follow Route 280 towards the Ober Gletschjoch till level with toe of the ridge at pt.2916m. Turn the first and second gendarmes on the N side, then follow the crest of the ridge to the foot of a large tower. Climb this by a difficult steep corner crack (pegs) and the next steep crack on the N side. Finally continue up the ridge without further incident to summit ($4\frac{1}{2}$–5h. from start).

Traverse of Dammazwillinge to Tiefenstock. *A splendid high level ridge climb from the Ober Gletschjoch (Route 279), following crest as much as possible, but avoiding difficulties if so*

desired or if necessary on the N side, to join the Tiefenstock S.
ridge (Route 131). III/IV (8–9h. from Ober Gletschjoch). First
traverse by Helene Kuntze with J. and G. Lochmatter in the early
1900s.

RHONESTOCK

This impressive rock mtn. lies N of the Tiefenstock and S of
the Dammastock. It has three main summits; the Vorderer
(two tops) and Hinterer, but the N summit of the former is not
marked on map. There is a difference of 1m. in the two maps
and that of LK.25,000 is represented.

All the climbs with the exception of the SW ridge are
approached from the Damma hut, across the Damma glacier.
The rock is good and the routes enjoyable and worthwhile;
specially recommended is the traverse from the Unter Winterjoch over the Vorderer to the Hinterer Rhonestock. The SW
ridge is uninteresting with far too long an approach for a climb
of so little merit. It could be used by those wishing to make a
long alternative descent to the Furka pass.

VORDERER RHONESTOCK   3566(3567)m.

South Summit (South Ridge). *A short interesting climb*
best done as part of the complete traverse. IV—. *First ascent*
R. Helbling, H. Biehly and Alb. Weber, 8 August, 1901.

144. From the Unter Winterjoch (Route 134) follow the ridge
to a series of steep slabs. Avoid these by taking a ledge on to
the W side, then climb an obvious dièdre to the ridge above,
which is followed to summit (1¼–2h. from joch).

South Summit (East Rib). *A good direct route.* IV—. *First*
ascent: A. Amstad and H. Flachsmann, 27 July, 1947. Diagram,
p.88.

145. From the Damma glacier take the well-defined rock rib
rising from snow immediately N, under the Unter Winterjoch.
To reach the lower rocks either cross the schrund to the S or N

of the rib, according to where it can be best taken. Avoid the
first part of the steep middle section to the R, then follow the
rib steeply to top (4–5h. from the start).

North Summit (South Ridge). *An excellent climb on perfect
rock.* III. *First ascent: Marcel Kurz, Oscar Hug and Anton Simmon,
23 September, 1917. Diagram, p.88.*

146. From the S summit (Vorderer) follow the exposed serrated
ridge and climb over four gendarmes. It is best to abseil from
the last two, then continue to summit (3h. from S summit).

North Summit (East Rib). *A recommendable climb, comparable
with the other routes.* III. *First ascent: A. Amstad and Hans
Flachsmann, 17 August, 1947. Diagram, p.88.*

147. Take the most southerly of two prominent rock ribs
descending to the Damma glacier immediately S of the Ober
Winterjoch. Start on S side of the lower rocks. Turn the first
steep section to the R (N) then return to the crest where the
rock is best. Continue up the steep rib to meet the main ridge
between the two summits (Route 146) (3h. from start).

It is also possible to follow the northerly rib. This is harder
and does not really offer better climbing (Alfred and Otto
Amstad, 5 August, 1945).

Descent from North Summit to Ober Winterjoch.
Descended by first ascensionists, 1947. Diagram, p.88.

148. From the summit descend slabs on the W wall, then,
when possible, traverse horizontally across to reach the joch.
The best and quickest means of descent is by abseiling.

HINTERER RHONESTOCK   3596(3595)m.

The immediate northerly neighbour of the Vorderer. Not such
an interesting or important mtn. It is best climbed as part of a
traverse of the three summits. First ascent: W. Vischer and
A. von der Muhli with J. Tresch, 22 July, 1867.

South Ridge. *A short interesting route, usually used for travers* *ing. I/II. First descended by A. Hitz, H. Kuhn, Fr. Müller an* *W. Rytz, 3 August, 1906. Diagram, p.88.*

149. From the Ober Winterjoch (see below) climb a steep chimney, then follow the easy rocky ridge to summit (30 min from joch).

Traverse from Unter Winterjoch to Rhonejoch. *A* *excellent climb on good rock; splendid situations; the bes* *route in the group. IV—. Diagram, p.88.*

150. From the Unter Winterjoch (Route 134) follow the S ridge (Route 144) to the Vorderer, and continue along the S ridge (Route 146) to N summit. Descend the N ridge (Route 148) to the Ober Winterjoch. Climb the S ridge (Route 149) to the Hinterer and finally descend N ridge to the Rhonejoch (Route 151) (6–8h. from joch to joch).

OBER WINTERJOCH   c.3535m.

Marked on LK.1:25,000. The deepest depression between the Vorderer and Hinterer Rhonestocks. From the E and W it is reached by two steep snow/ice couloirs guarded by berg schrunds. Both couloirs are objectively dangerous; on the E side from the Damma glacier it is best to follow rocks to the N and on the W side the southerly rocks. It is rarely used as a pass, merely as a means of access or retreat for the Rhone stock. This is also limited as most parties continue across to the Rhonestock. First crossing: Max Comte and three com panions, 19 August, 1900. This party took 8h. from bergschrund on the E (Damma) side.

RHONEJOCH   c.3520m.

Marked on LK.1:25,000. The deepest depression between the Hinterer Rhonestock and pt.3549m. This pt. is immediately S of the Damma pass. It is rarely used as a pass but as a means of access to the Rhonestock–Dammastock ridge. The W side is a long, easy skiing route over the upper névés of the Rhone glacier. First ascent: Marcel Kurz and Anton Simmen, 14 July, 1918.

151. From the Damma hut follow Route 152 to below the Damma pass, then continue further SW to below the joch. Cross a bergschrund, not usually difficult, and climb straight up a large snow couloir to top. This is quick and pleasant in good snow conditions, and is not too steep (3h. from hut to bergschrund; 1h. from there to joch). *Diagram, p.88.*

DAMMA PASS c.3500m.

A snow pass between pts.3549m. and 3506m. (LK.1:25,000) and to the immediate N of the Rhonejoch. Easy from the W, but a serious undertaking from the E. The Damma glacier can be complicated and the final step to the pass can be very tricky in icy conditions. First crossing: A. Hoffmann–Burckhardt with Ulrich Lauener and a porter, 1 August, 1868.

From the East.

152. From the Damma hut follow the track running S of the Mosstock to reach the Damma glacier. Go W below pt.2811m. then traverse SW to the foot of a distinct snowy rib descending from the Dammastock E wall. (The line across the glacier is confused by broken ice and crevasses to L and R). From below the rib slant up SW (crevasses) to foot of the steep couloir which rises to the pass, wide at the bottom, narrowing at top. Cross the bergschrund; then climb either a rock rib rising to the subsidiary peak at pt.3549m., S of the pass, and finally descend or traverse to the pass; or climb the couloir direct, the quickest route but only recommended in good conditions; or climb rocks on the N side of couloir. This latter course is unpleasant and the least recommended (4–5h. from hut).

From the West.

153. From the upper Rhone glacier the pass is reached without complications over easy névés. This is long and more suitable for skiing.

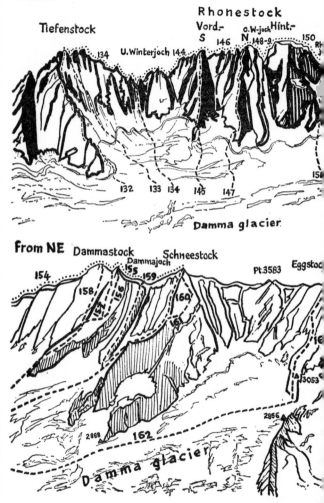

from E

Tiefenstock

Rhonestock

Vord.-S 146   o.W-joch Hint.-

U.Winterjoch 144   146   148-9   150 Rh

134

132 133 134   145   147

Damma glacier

from NE Dammastock   Schneestock

Dammajoch

154   155   159   Pt.3583   Eggstoc

158   156   160

157   161

3053

2888   162   2886

Damma glacier

DAMMASTOCK   3629.9m.

A twin summited peak; the highest mtn. in this part of the Alps. The western aspect is one of easy névés, but that from the E one of savage rock and ice scenery, involving climbs of a serious mountaineering nature. An important feature to be faced on the ridge and E face routes is the enormous cornice which can make climbs from this side quite dangerous and descent awkward. First ascent: A. Hoffmann–Burckhardt with A. von Weissenfluh and Joh. Fischer, 28 July, 1864. This party approached the mtn. from the W side over the névés of the Upper Rhone glacier. This is seldom done today except on ski.

South Ridge. *An easy climb; a pleasant expedition if done with a traverse to the N summit and a descent of the N ridge to the Dammajoch. The main difficulties are the ascent to the Damma pass and the descent from the Dammajoch. I/II. Beware of cornice above the E wall. First ascent: C. Seelig and A. Näf with Jos Zgraggen and J. M. Gamma, 1908. Diagram, p.88.*

154. From the Damma hut follow Route 152 to the Damma pass then climb the easy snow ridge to main summit. The N summit is easily reached from here. (30 min. from pass).

North Ridge. *This is best taken as a descent route after traversing from the S ridge and main summit. The only complications are those on the Dammajoch. I/II. Diagram, p.88.*

155. From the Damma hut follow Route 159 to the Dammajoch, then climb the easy snow ridge to the N summit. Beware of cornice on the E (L) wall (20–30 min. from joch).

East Rib of North Summit. *A good combination climb; the best and hardest on the mtn. III. First ascent: C. Seelig with Jos. Zgraggen, 12 October, 1890. Diagram, p.88.*

156. From the Damma hut follow Route 152 on to the Damma glacier to below the distinct snow rib rising into the E wall. Climb this rib for about two-thirds of its height to below the wall. Traverse R across the foot of the snow/ice couloir which descends from the gap between the main and N summits. Cross slabby rock R to below the rock rib rising to the N summit.

Now climb slabs to reach the crest of the rib which is followed
to the top at a pt. where the summit cornice is smallest or
sometimes non-existent. Continue along the ridge easily to
main summit (5–6h. from hut).

East Rib to Main Summit. *A pleasant climb following a direct
route to summit. I/II. First ascent: Ed. Imhof and Albert Frei
6 August, 1919. Diagram, p. 88.*

158. From the top of the snow rib (Route 152) go L, then climb
the middle rib direct to top (2½h. from start).

If used for descent do not go too far R when descending
the rib.

DAMMAJOCH   c.3560m.

This pass lies between the Dammastock and Schneestock and
is used as a direct means of ascent or descent to or from the
high level ridge of the Dammastock-Schneestock. First ascent:
R. Helbling, R. Martin and E. Frankhauser, 6 July, 1902. *Diagram,
p.88.*

159. From the Damma hut follow Route 152 to below the snowy
rib. Now go up below this rib on the N side to foot of the couloir
which rises to the joch between the two summits. Cross the
bergschrund, then go L and join the rock rib which runs up
S (L) of the couloir. Climb this to top, keeping to its crest, and
avoiding difficulties to the R (N). This is safer than climbing
the couloir itself (2½–3h. from hut).

SCHNEESTOCK   3608m.

An impressive mtn. situated a short distance N of the Dammastock. The W side together with the N and S ridges is easy and
warrants no description, being identical to the approaches for
its southerly neighbour. The Damma side affords two difficult
and serious climbs. First ascent by N ridge: A. Hoffmann-
Burckhardt with Andreas von Weissenfluh and J. Fischer,
28 July, 1864.

East Edge. *The best and most difficult route on the mtn. Only slight danger from stone or icefall. V. First ascent: Alfred Amstad and Guido Masetto, 23 August, 1935. Diagram, p.88.*

160. From the Damma hut follow Route 152 below the snow rib, to a pt. below the couloir leading to the Dammajoch. Now bear R and reach the marked gap in the E ridge. Follow the ridge easily to the first barrier, which is turned on L by a scree-covered ledge. Climb directly back to the ridge which leads to a steep 'impasse'; the true start of the E *kante*. Climb straight up steep rock for about three rope-lengths, then turn an overhang by climbing out L on to the SE wall. Climb up delicately L for about 15m. to reach a ledge leading back to the ridge edge. It is now best to avoid the crest and climb the steep R side of the *kante*; difficult and exposed. Turn the last overhanging section on the N side, then regain the *kante* which is finally followed over snow to summit (8–10h. from hut).

North Wall. *A fairly difficult route and dangerous from stone and icefall. The summit cornice which is often enormous threatens the whole face. It is seldom done. IV. First ascent: M. Kurz and H. Neumeyer, 1917. Diagram, p.88.*

161. Follow Route 152 to the steep buttress which marks the start of the true E *kante*, then follow a narrow scree-covered ledge to its end, leading out on to the N face. Now climb good rock to a crack which slants R. Follow this to the top (pegs), then make a difficult tricky step R to a second crack which leads to a slab. Climb to a downwards projecting peak of rock, pass under this, then go steeply upwards. Finally mount progressively easier rocks, trend L to the E ridge and follow this to summit (6–7h. from hut).

Descent. *For both these routes the most practical descent is the easy S ridge (cornice) down to the Dammajoch, thence to the Damma hut (Route 159) (1½–2h.).*

MOSSTOCK   2611m.

A long rock ridge running behind the Damma hut. The climbing is not difficult; it provides something to do in bad weather.

DAMMAPLATTEN   2811m.

This sharp narrow ridge situated W of and connected to the Mosstock is unnamed on map; if combined with a traverse from the latter it affords a splendid training climb on excellent rock. The way is from E to W, and join the Damma glacier just after passing pt. 2498m. (LK.1:25,000). IV. (5–6h. from hut).

EGGSTOCK   3582., 3554m.

A twin-headed peak NW of the Schneestock, the last important mtn. on the Dammastock high level ridge. The S and W ridges are easy, but the approaches are long and rarely done from the Damma side. Neither the N face nor the NE ridge can be recommended; the rock is bad, the climbing poor and on the former route there is a fair amount of objective danger. Only the E wall really merits description; the SW flank from the Upper Rhone glacier is best done on ski. First ascent: Gottlieb Wenger with A. von Weissenfluh, 7 July, 1884.

East Wall. *An interesting climb, the best on the mtn., but the glacier approach can be difficult and should only be attempted in the best conditions. II, but serious of its class. First ascent: Marcel Kurz and Anton Simmen, 14 July, 1918. Diagram, p.88.*

162. From the Damma hut follow Route 152 over the Damma glacier to where the Dammaplatten merges into the snow. Go N and descend about 50m. to a large broken crevasse system; then climb NW (crevasses) to pt. 2856m. at the foot of a distinct rock rib running up into the E wall. Climb W and get on to the rib by reaching a small shoulder. Continue over snow and rock on to the E wall. Climb a couloir which is parallel with the NE ridge (R). Finally go up steep rocks to the main summit (4–5h. from hut).

WISSNOLLEN   3398.2m.

A splendid small snow peak rising above the Eggfirn and Triftsach; W of Eggstock and NE of the Ober Triftlimmi. A number of easy routes exist but the most practical and enjoyable is the NW ridge, descending towards the Trift kessel to pt. 3083m. (LK. 1:25,000). The easiest route is to follow the E side of the SW ridge (entirely snow) from the Ober Triftlimmi (Route 83). From the summit the broad easy snow ridge can be followed E to the Eggstock (Gottlieb Wenger with A. von Weissenfluh, 7 July, 1884). First ascent: Th. Simmler with two guides, 1862 (SW ridge).

North-West Ridge. *A pleasant easy mixed ridge.* I. *First ascent:
H. O. S. Gibson and L. R. C. Sommer, 15 August, 1910.*

163. From the Trift hut follow Route 83 up the Unter Trift Kessel, thence S to the Ober Trift Kessel. At c.3000m. go E and join the ridge at pt. 3083m.; then follow it over snow and easy rocks to summit (2½–3h. from Trift hut).

TRIFTGRAT   3385m., 3372m., 3341m. (LK.1:25,000–3387m., 3379., 3347m.)

A sharp rock ridge between the Eggstock and S Maasplankjoch (Route 167). The rock on the crest is poor and the traverse cannot be recommended. The E ridges of pts. 3372(9)m. and 3341(7)m. are good and difficult but the approach from the Kehlenalp hut is quite difficult (crevassed) and long. First ascent of pt. 3372(9)m. on E ridge: Carl Seelig with J. Zgreggen, 15 July, 1888. First ascent of pt. 3385(7)m: R. Helbling with Peter Mattli, 20 July, 1904.

PART III

TIERBERG GROUP

A small compact area situated NE of the Tieralplistock group. To the N is the beautiful Gadmental, to the S the great icefields of the Trift and Kehlen glaciers. None of the climbing is difficult, but the routes on the central massif of the Hinter and Vorder Tierberg have a sense of serious mountaineering in magnificent surroundings.

Several good, direct and relatively easy passes such as the Steinlimmi, Zwischen Tierbergen and S and N Maasplankjoch connect the area with other mtn. groups and huts. The Windegg, Trift, Kehlenalp and Tierbergli huts are conveniently placed and serve adequately. The hotel at Steinglacier on the Susten pass, which is open from June to September, is well situated for several mtn. ascents and passes.

MAASPLANKSTOCK   3401.2m.

An impressive rock peak, rising above the snowfields of the Trift glacier to the W and the Kehlen glacier to the E. The climbs are short and interesting but involve fairly long glacier work, requiring a degree of experience.

South Ridge. *An easy route, best used for descent in a traverse along the N ridge. I. First ascent: Heinrich Dübi, Fritz Wyss, Otto Hopf and August Rätzer with Jon and Andreas von Weissenfluh, 8 July, 1872.*

164. From the Trift hut follow Route 167 to the S Maasplankjoch. Go up the lower broken part of the ridge, then climb the crest on better rock, turning a small tower easily on W (L) side and reach the top without further difficulty (4–4½h. from hut).

North Ridge. *An interesting climb on good rock, the best on the mtn. II/III, or easier depending on route chosen. First ascent:*

R. von Wyss, A. Hügli, W. Baumgarter and August Plüss, 6 August, 1894.

65. From the Trift hut follow Route 169 to the N Maasplankjoch. Turn the first large rock tower on the W (R) side, then keep to crest of the deeply-serrated ridge, turning difficulties as necessary on the W (R) side, and climb to summit ($3\frac{1}{2}$–4h. from hut).

East Wall. *A fairly good combination route, seldom done.* II+. First descended by R. Helbling and G. B. Litscher, 22 July, 1899.

66. From the Kehlenalp hut follow Route 168 to the Maasplankfirn. Climb the S (L) side of a distinct snow gully rising towards the S ridge. Traverse R to a second couloir, and then further to join a rocky rib leading to summit. Follow this keeping a little below the crest to the top. Sometimes the bergschrund can be difficult to cross (4–5h.).

SOUTH MAASPLANKJOCH 3300m.

The deepest gap in ridge between the Maasplankstock (3401.2m.) (LK.1:50,000) and pt. 3326m. (LK.1:25,000). A useful pass between the Trift and Kehlenalp huts. Both sides are glaciated, but the (E) Kehlenalp side is steeper and more difficult. II. First crossing: E. J. Häberlin and E. Zugler with Joh. and Andreas von Weissenfluh, 26 August, 1868.

67. From the Trift hut go S to reach the Unter Triftkessel; then work SE towards the rock rib descending from the Wiss Nollen (3398.2m.) into the glacier. Pass L of this rib and reach the level upper firn of the Triftsach. From the Unter Triftkessel it is more direct to ascend E, keeping R below the rocks of pt. 2768m., but this is more crevassed. From the Triftsach go to the foot of the rock rib descending from pt. 3322m. (3326m. LK.1:25,000). Immediately NW there is an obvious snowy bay. Climb easy scree covered rocks at the back of this bay to the pass ($1\frac{1}{2}$–2h. from hut).

168. From the Kehlenalp hut descend SW past pt. 2127.8m into the Kehlenalptal. Cut across the bottom of the narrow valley in the same direction to below steep rocks of the Schatt migstock. Avoid the rocks by going L up steep grass. As soon as possible bear R and cross the rocky rib which descends from pt. 3341m. (3344m. LK.1:25,000). Make a short descent over rocks to the Maasplankfirn, then cross snow NW till below the pass, which lies just NW of pt. 3322m. (3326m LK.1:25,000). Climb a snowy gully; the bergschrund can some times be very wide and awkward, then finally over moderately difficult rocks to pass (2½–3h. from hut).

NORTH MAASPLANKJOCH   c.3350m.

Between the Maasplankstock and pt. 3352m. A far more difficult proposition than its southerly counterpart and consequently not so popular. II/III. First crossing: Legh S. Powell with Heinrich Zurflüh, 19 July, 1901.

169. From the Trift hut follow Route 167 to below pt. 2768m Go further E past this pt. and reach the foot of a prominent snow couloir. Climb this steep couloir and at the top emerge on crest of a snow ridge which is followed to the pass. An easier but somewhat longer route is to continue nearly as high as the snow bay (Route 167), then climb NW over fairly gentle snow slopes to pass (2½–3h. from hut).

170. From the Kehlenalp hut descend to reach the Kehler glacier, which is followed NW past pt. 2623m., the foot of a rock rib which descends E from the Maasplankstock. Now slant W over the glacier (crevasses) to reach two distinct wide and steep couloirs. Climb either of these to the pass (3–3½h.).

HINTER TIERBERG   3447m., 3443.5m., 3418m. and c.3300m.

A long complicated mtn.; a rocky ridge with several different summit pts. To avoid confusion each pt. is treated as a separate summit. Overall it is an impressive peak with magnificent views. Most of the climbing is fairly easy and short, being close to the Trift hut. Better and longer climbs can be had by combining different routes.

South Summit   pt. 3447m.

South Ridge. *An easy and interesting climb. I/II. First ascent: Legh S. Powell with Heinrich Zurflüh, 1901.*

171. From the N Maasplankjoch (Routes 169/170) follow crest of the rocky ridge over pts. 3352m. and 3358m. to summit (2–3h.).

South-West Wall. *An easy snow climb, ideal for a quick descent. A few crevasses are easily avoided. I. First descent: Legh S. Powell and Frank Gare, 29 August, 1891.*

172. From the Trift hut work round SE over the glacier, then up snow NE to summit. Usually the final part is over easy rocks (2½h. from hut).

North Ridge. *A short pleasant climb. I/II. First ascent: Legh S. Powell and Frank Gare, 29 August, 1891.*

173. From the main summit, pt. 3443.5m. (see Route 174) follow crest of the ridge to pt. 3447m. (40 min. from pt. 3443.5m.). The climb can also be done from a marked gap in the ridge between the two summits. An easy straightforward gully runs down to the Trift glacier, and can be soon reached from Routes 172 and 174.

Main Summit   3443.5m.
Although not the highest this is the trig. pt.

South-West Flank. *An easy snow climb, popular on ski. I.*
174. From the Trift hut follow Route 172 to below the S summit then climb directly up a snowfield to top (2½–3h., depending on snow conditions).

South Ridge. *An easy climb, best done with a traverse from S summit. Can also be started from gap in the ridge between the two summits (Route 173). I/II. First descent: Legh S. Powell and Frank Gare, 29 August, 1891.*

175. From S summit or gap in the ridge follow the crest without difficulty to top (30–40 min.).

West Ridge. *An interesting climb starting directly from the hut, and convenient for those who dislike crevassed glaciers. I/II First ascent: G. L. Gerster with Joh. v. Weissenfluh, 3 August, 1850.*

176. From the Trift hut climb the rocky ridge which rises NE to reach an obvious snow ridge. Follow this W, finally over somewhat broken rock to summit (3h. from hut).

NORTH MITTLERER TIERBERG I   pt.3418m.

North-West Ridge (from Tierbergsattel). *A short climb, best done while crossing the pass (Routes 183/184). I. Can be more difficult if icy. First ascent: J. and A. von Weissenfluh, 1 August, 1864.*

177. From the Tierberg sattel (Route 183) follow the narrow snow ridge and finally easy rocks to summit (30min. from sattel).

South Ridge. *The best and hardest climb on the mtn. Good rock. Unfortunately to do this climb from the Trift hut it is necessary to descend the N ridge from pt.3443.5m. which is extremely loose, quite difficult and very unpleasant. III. First ascent: W. Gysin and O. Lienhard, 25 July, 1937.*

178. From the Kehlenalp hut go NW up the Kehlen glacier (crevasses) to the upper névés below a deep cut in the ridge between pts. 3443.5m. and 3418m. Climb to this gap, not difficult but loose, then follow the S ridge to summit (4–4½h. from hut).

NORTH MITTLERER TIERBERG II c.3340m.

Not marked on LK. Merely a shoulder of the N Mittlerer Tierberg I.

East Flank. *A pure snow climb, good on ski.* I. *First ascent: Thomas Brooksbank and R. N. Hayward with Kaspar Blatter and Fritz Ogi, 24 August, 1866.*

179. From the Tierberglimmi (Routes 183/184) climb fairly steep snow to summit (15–20min.).

South Ridge. *A short detour while crossing the Tierberg sattel.* I. *First ascent: O. Schär and a companion, 5 August, 1903.*

180. From the sattel reach the summit in about 10min.

North-East Wall. *The most interesting route on the mtn. Excellent practice on steep ice.* II/III, *depending on snow conditions. First ascensionists in descent.*

181. From pt. 2991m., just NE of the Zwischen Tierbergen pass (Routes 185/186), climb the steep ice wall direct, then over easier névé to summit (1–1½h.).

North Ridge. *This route can be unjustifiably unpleasant and difficult when icy. Normal icy conditions in the upper sections make it tricky.* II/III, *depending on conditions. First ascent: Fred. Gardiner with Rudi and Peter Almer, 23 July, 1905.*

182. From the Zwischen Tierbergen pass (Routes 185/186) follow a short snow ridge leading to rocks which form the N face. Climb these, usually icy and delicate, to summit (1½–2h.).

TIERBERGSATTEL c.3300m.

A small saddle situated N of pt. 3418m. (N Mittlerer Tierberg I). Useful as a pass between the Windegg, Trift and Tierbergli huts; it gives a first-class expedition on rock and ice. I/II. First ascent from NE: A. Hoffmann-Burckhardt with Andreas von Weissenfluh and Joh Fischer, 29 July, 1864. First traverse: Legh S. Powell and Walter Larden, 22 August, 1902.

183. From the W. From the Trift hut descend a short distanc
NW to reach the foot of the Zwischen Tierberg glacier. This p
can be reached from the Windegg hut by crossing the Windeg
ridge and crossing the Trift glacier to SE.

Ascend the N (L) moraine to c.2400m., then rise across
(SE) to meet the foot of a rock ridge which descends from th
summit ridge N of pt.3418m. Climb this ridge, past pt.2648m
to the top of the pass (5–6h. from Trift or Windegg huts).

184. From the E. From the Tierberglimmi (Route 187) work u
and round to SW over snow to the saddle (10–20min.).

ZWISCHEN TIERBERGEN   2991m.

A snow saddle between the N Mittlerer Tierberg I (pt.3418m.)
and the Vorder Tierberg (3094m.). The most direct pass fron
Stein in the Upper Gadmental via the Tierbergli hut to the
Trift hut. Technically an easy route, but quite a serious glacie
expedition. Sometimes the crevasses can be very difficult
First crossing: Alb Hoffmann-Burckhardt with A. vor
Weissenfluh and Joh. Fischer, 29 July, 1864. *Diagram, p.102.*

185. From the E. From the Tierbergli hut go SW, descending
slightly, keeping just above the icefall of the Steinlimm
glacier, then climb to the pass. (40–50min.).

186. From the W. From the Windegg or Trift huts follow
Route 183 to the 2400m. contour. Depending on conditions
or choice, either continue up the moraine which eventually
merges into the upper snows, then bear NE to top of the pass;
or climb the glacier itself direct to the pass (4–5h. from either
hut).

TIERBERGLIMMI (KEHLENJOCH or KEHLENLÜCKE)
3202m.

A snow saddle between the Mittlerer Tierberg and the
Gwächtenhorn. Too variable in conditions and difficulties

o be popular. It is always badly crevassed and in bad conditions is unjustifiably complicated for a relatively unimportant
pass. First crossing: A. Hoffmann-Burckhardt with Andreas
. Weissenfluh and Joh. Fischer, 31 July, 1864. *Diagram, p.102.*

187. From the NE. From the Tierbergli hut climb towards the
foot of the Gwächtenhorn NE ridge, then SW over the badly
crevassed glacier to the pass (1h. or longer, depending on
state of the crevasses).

188. From the SE. From the Kehlenalp hut ascend the Kehlenalp glacier, keeping to the N side past two badly crevassed
and broken areas, then move into the centre of the glacier to
reach the foot of a wide couloir leading to the pass above.
Either climb this gully as directly as possible, sometimes very
difficult (broken and crevassed); or better still take a gully on
the R (E) side which rises to the ridge above. The pass can
be easily reached from here (4–5h. from hut).

VORDER TIERBERG   3094m.

A fine rock and ice peak with some splendid climbing. The
best routes are approached from Stein in the Upper
Gadmental.

South-East Flank. *A short, easy route. Good for descent but
well worth climbing while crossing the Zwischen Tierbergen
pass. I. First descent: F. Baker-Gabb and his wife, 23 July, 1898.*
189. From the Zwischen Tierbergen pass (Routes 185/186)
follow the ridge on the L or go somewhat below to the R over
easy névé to reach summit (30 min. from pass).

North-East Ridge. *One of the finest and most impressive
ridges in the Tierberg group. Predominately rocky, with a delicate
snow/ice section at the top. II/III. First ascent: Bernhard Lauterburg
and Hans Morgenthaler, 3 September, 1916. Diagram, p.102.*
190. Follow Route 193 towards the Steinlimmi pass and join
the ridge at the lowest pt. where it projects into the centre of the

Tierberg NE side

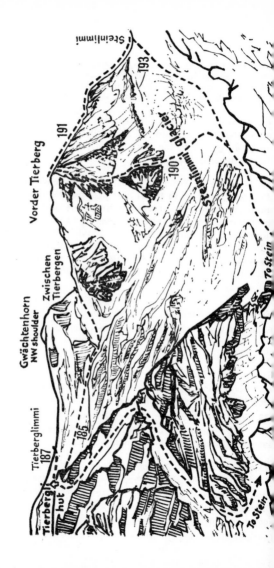

Steinlimmi

193

191

190

Vorder Tierberg

Steinlimmi glacier

Zwischen Tierbergen

Gwächtenhorn
NW shoulder

Tierberglimmi
187

185

Tierbergli
hut

To Stein

To Stein

glacier. Climb the central rib of the somewhat indefinite lower spur; this is followed by a more horizontal serrated crest. Follow the steep rock ridge directly above and at the top move R and climb the steep sharp snow ice ridge. When it eases, keep to the ridge (sometimes corniced) and bear WNW to the highest pt. (2–3h. from start).

North-West Ridge. *An interesting varied climb with splendid views.* II. *First ascent: W. Baumgartner and H. Schneider. Diagram, p.102.*

191. Follow Route 193 nearly to the top of the Steinlimmi pass. Before this pt. slant L (WSW) over steep snow/ice, crossing at least two bergschrunds to reach the ridge. Follow this to summit (2½–3h. from Steinlimmi).

North-West Ridge (from Windegg hut). *A good climb, but inferior and easier than the approach from Steinlimmi.* I/II.

192. From the hut follow Route 186 for the Zwischen Tierbergen pass to a pt. where the N moraine merges into the upper névé, Now bear up L across the glacier to the deepest gap in ridge, between pt.2999m. and the summit; easily recognised by a prominent red gendarme. From here follow the ridge to summit (5–6h. from hut).

STEINLIMMI   2734m.

A pass between the Vorder Tierberg and the Giglistock. The most direct and easiest route between Stein and the Windegg hut. Also useful for the Trift hut as an alternative to the Zwischen Tierbergen. I. First crossing: Gottlieb Studer with Peter Baumann and Joh. von Weissenfluh, 8 August, 1841. *Diagram, p.102.*

193. From Stein follow Route 4 for the Tierbergli hut, as far as the Steinlimmi glacier. Now follow the glacier directly to the pass. A few crevasses at the foot of the V. Tierberg NE ridge (2½–3h. from Stein).

194. From Windegg hut. Follow the path across the Windegg ridge and traverse the Trift glacier ENE to the Drosi torrent. Go up the narrow valley beside the torrent to reach the névé of the upper cwm formed by the Vorder Tierberg and Giglistock. Cross snow ENE and climb a scree-filled gully with two rocky steps to the pass (3–4h. from hut).

GIGLISTOCK   2900m.

A pleasant snow/ice peak N of the Vorder Tierberg. To the NE it overlooks the Upper Gadmental and has splendid views towards the Titlis group.

South-East Flank. *A somewhat laborious, easy snow route; interesting on ski.* I. *First ascent: H. Baumgartner with Joh. Tännler and G. Linder, 17 July, 1891.*

195. Follow Route 193 from Stein to the Steinlimmi glacier. When just past the foot of the Vorder Tierberg NE ridge, slant R (NW) over easy rock or snow, then over easy névé to summit (3½–4h. from Stein).

South Ridge. *A good interesting route, the best on the mtn.* II/III. *First ascent: Legh S. Powell and J. A. Hutchinson, 1 August, 1884.*

196. From the Steinlimmi pass (Route 193) climb the ridge, rocky, at first, finally snow to summit (1½–2h. from pass).

East and North-West Ridges. *Neither of these ridges is technically difficult, but the approach is long and remote over the Taleggli glacier (crevasses). One of the best combinations is to ascend the E Ridge and descend the NW, or alternatively to descend to the Windegg hut (Route 200).*

North-West Ridge. *Fairly interesting but seldom climbed; it is recommended to take in the peak of pt.2853.5m.* I. *First ascent from pt.2853m.: Paul Baumgartner and Hans v. Rütte, 25 August, 1912.*

197. From Stein slant up W to pt.2053.9m. Work round to SW to a small lake, pt.2056m., at Taleggi, then go up a small valley (W) with a stream. Follow this valley to the Taleggi glacier. Go W across the glacier (large crevasses in centre, icefall to R) to the saddle S (L) to pt.2853.5m. or join the ridge N of this pt. Follow the ridge to summit. Pt.2853.5m. can also be reached from the Windegg hut by following Route 200 to the saddle and up its W ridge (4–5h. from Stein).

East Ridge. *More interesting than the NW with a shorter uncomplicated glacier approach. Recommended for ascent.* I.

198. Follow Route 197 to the Taleggli glacier, then climb N to the saddle W of the Brunnenstock; an obvious rock peak. Now follow the easy-angled ridge, either on the crest or on the snow, to summit (3½–4h.).

BRUNNENSTOCK 2763m.

An impressive rocky peak forming a great buttress at the end of the Giglistock E ridge, but separated from the latter by a saddle.

West Ridge. *An easy climb and the only practical one on the mtn. The impressive E ridge is far too shattered, broken and loose to justify any climbing.* I. *First ascent: Legh S. Powell, W. V. Compton, A. V. Valentine-Richards and T. H. Fitzpatrick, 4 September, 1908.*

199. From Stein follow Route 198 to the saddle at the start of the Giglistock E ridge. From here follow the ridge easily to summit (3–3½h. from Stein).

WANGHÖRNER 2354m., 2542m., 2796m., 2819m., and 2835m.

A long mtn. ridge running N–S with several summit points; and lying NW of the Giglistock. The mtn. can be approached from either the Windegg hut or Stein; both routes are fairly long, in wild lonely surroundings. In bad weather special care should be exercised in the descent to the Windegg hut.

From Windegg hut. *Easy but worthwhile.* I. *First ascent: F. Baker-Gabb and his wife, 15 July, 1898.*

200. From the hut follow Route 194 to the glacier below the Steinlimmi pass. Go directly N past pt.2570m. into a large glacier cwm and keep in the same direction, up to a gap in the ridge between pts.2835m. (N) and 2853.5m. (WNW). Follow the ridge W to pt.2835m. then NW to pt.2819m. (4–5h. from hut).

Descent. Either descend the Gigli glacier from pt. 2819m. and thence E to Stein (Route 197); or return along the ridge to pt. 2838m., then follow Route 202 along N ridge to the Drosistock, with a descent of the NW flank (Route 203) to join the original route from Windegg hut.

From Stein. *A fairly long approach but interesting.* I. *First ascent: Legh S. Powell, W. C. Compton, A. V. Valentine-Richards and T. H. Fitzpatrick, 7 September, 1908.*

201. Go W by Miser, descending slightly to Lischen, pt.1811m. Keep in the same direction across Alp Gigli then climb S to reach the Gigli glacier. Climb this almost to the top, then move R and ascend easy rocks to join the N ridge which is followed to pt. 2819m. (5–6h. from Stein).

DROSISTOCK   2821m.

A small rock peak S of the Wanghörner. Rarely climbed for its own sake, but usually taken in conjunction with its northerly neighbour.

North Ridge (from Wanghörner, pt.2835m.). *Short and easy.* I. *First ascent: F. Baker-Gabb and his wife, 15 July, 1898.*

202. From pt.2835m. (Route 200) follow the ridge to summit (30min).

North-West Flank. *Tedious and loose in ascent but useful for descending.* I/II *First ascent: Paul Baumgartner and Hans v. Rütte, 25 August, 1912.*

203. From the Windegg hut follow Route 200 to the narrow valley which leads to the Steinlimmi pass. At about half height by Drosi, at c.2180m., slant L (NE) and climb into the Trümmer kessel; the cwm formed by the Gadenlauihorn (pt.2776m.), Wanghorn and Drosistock. From the cwm go SE and climb loose broken rock of the NW flank to summit (3–4h. from hut).

GRAUE STÖCKLI   2714m.

GADENLAUIHORN   2776m.

MURMETENSTOCK   2609m.

RADLEFSHORN   2603m.

SONNIGHORN or **DOGGELISTEIN**   2399m.

This cluster of small peaks and ridges lies W of the Giglistock and NE of the Windegg hut. There is little or no climbing, but they are good viewpoints and can be easily ascended from any side; the Windegg being preferable for the height advantage. Some easy and good ridge scrambling combinations can be worked out by the more imaginative.

PART IV

SUSTENHORN GROUP

This group forms a long ridge running N–SE. The Sustenspitz to the N dominates the head of the Susten pass; the Grand-schijen in the SE overlooks the upper Göschenertal.

This is an ideal area for the experienced climber and the novice. Several serious combination climbs are to be found on the Sustenhorn and Kl. Sustenhorn, together with a good selection of easy, normal, and interesting routes. Both these mtns. are surrounded by large glaciers, adding a degree of complication to the uninitiated. The rock is generally good with the notable exception of the Sustenspitz, which is loose and untrustworthy.

The mtns. centred round the Bergseeschijen in the Göschenertal are for the more specialist rock climber; they provide technical routes on excellent granite, nearly all of them of a high standard. The building of the Bergsee hut and the easy access to the heart of this group by road from Göschenen has made it a very popular climbing ground, especially at weekends.

Other huts serving the area are the Tierbergli, Kehlenalp and Voralp, all of which are interconnected by a series of easy and frequented passes such as the Kehlenalplücke and Sustenlimmi.

SUSTENSPITZ   2930.8m.

A sharp impressive rock peak dominating the top of the Susten pass. The climbing is not good, owing to bad rock; the two best and most frequented routes are described below. It is a fine viewpoint and well worth the effort involved, being so close to the road.

North-East Ridge. *An easy ridge, equally popular for ascent or descent. I/II. First ascent: E. F. M. Benecke and H. V. Reade, 30 July, 1893. Diagram, p.112.*

204. From the top of the pass climb to join the ridge at any convenient spot and follow it to summit (2h.).

North-West Ridge. *A fairly popular climb; usually done as a normal route. Tricky when wet.* II. *Diagram, p.112.*

205. From the top of the pass go to the foot of the ridge and follow this taking the best line whenever possible, either on the ridge or the face to the top ($2\frac{1}{2}$–3h.).

SUSTENJOCH   2656m.

Between the Kl. Sustenhorn and Stucklistock, joining the Voralp (S) and Chalch (N) valleys. Easy from the S but fairly difficult and unpleasant on the N side. II/III. First crossing; Gottlieb Studer with Heinrich Glaus, 22 July, 1840. *Diagram, p.112.*

206. From the S. From the Voralp hut ascend NW keeping on the E (R) side of the Wallenburfirn (glacier), then climb steepening snow and finally rocks to pass ($1\frac{1}{2}$–2h.).

207. From the N. From the Chalchtal, just below the top of the Susten pass (E side), go directly towards a steep wall which descends from the pass. Climb over scree and steep broken rocks, often snow-covered, keeping in a line somewhat W (R) of the pass; finally traverse L to top of the joch ($1\frac{1}{2}$–2h.).

KLEIN SUSTENHORN   N Summit 3315m., S Summit 3308m.

A large rocky mtn. S of the Sustenspitz. The climbs are quite long and serious with a fair amount of glacier work when approached from the Voralp side.

East Wall (to N summit). *A good snow/ice route; the usual route from the Voralp hut.* I/II. *First ascent:* W. Gröbli with Joseph M. Gamma, 6 August, 1891. *Diagram, p.112.*

208. From the Voralp hut follow Route 206 to the upper névé of the Wallenburfirn, past pt.2536m. Now go L (W) below pt.2576m., up into the glacier cwm below the E wall of the two summits. Take the third and most northerly of three rocky ribs which descend in a line with the S summit, and climb on the R side of this rib on steep snow. Continue upwards over snow, bearing R; the slope narrows to form a sort of wide couloir. From the connecting ridge of the two summits a triangular-shaped area of rock descends into the upper snow-field. Climb to the R below these rocks, then to the summit, either keeping to the snow or bearing L onto ridge ($4\frac{1}{2}$–5h.).

East Wall (to S summit). *A good interesting route, more variable than Route 208; can be difficult and dangerous in bad weather.* II. First ascent: G. End, August, 1899. Diagram, p.112.

209. From the Voralp hut follow Route 208 into the glacier cwm. Take the middle rock rib, separated by a snow couloir from the third, northerly one, and climb this on the L side, L of a small snow gully. As soon as possible slant up R and join the crest of the rib. Follow this crest and at about half height traverse R over rocks above the R-hand snow couloir to reach the un-broken snow slopes below the rocks of the SE ridge. Cross these snow slopes, keeping below the rock, up to a gully in the summit wall. Follow this to the top, bearing somewhat L near the summit ($4\frac{1}{2}$–5h.).

North-East Ridge. *A fine climb; not difficult but fairly steep at the top.* II. First ascent: Val. A. Fynn and Enk. E. Kengran, 22 July, 1894. Diagram, p.112.

210. From the Voralp hut follow Route 206 to the Sustenjoch, then climb the ridge to the top. The key pitch is the upper section, climbed by a crack; it can also be turned on the S side (L) when snow conditions are good. (3h. from Sustenjoch).

In descent, a couloir which starts half-way up the ridge can be descended easily to the glacier cwm just above the upper névé of the Wallenburfirn. This can also be used in ascent, as a short cut, but is not so aesthetic.

North-West Ridge. *A fairly difficult and interesting climb; the best route on the N or W sides. It can be used in descent from a traverse over the S summit or Sustenhorn, but the main draw-*

back is that the climber from the Voralp hut ends up on the wrong side of the Sustenjoch. III. First ascent: E. Labhardt, F. Grob and E. Armberg with a porter, J. Zgraggen, 27 August, 1899. Diagram, p.112.

211. From the Chalchtallücke (Route 214) follow the ridge for the first 200m. without difficulty to the first steep section; this is avoided by a couloir on the N (L) side. Take a second couloir, and finally climb difficult rocks to rejoin crest of the ridge. Follow this for some way, to c.3000m., then turn a tower on the W (R) side. Continue on the ridge for some distance, and below the summit block traverse on to the N side and climb L to the top, usually up a snow-filled gully (5h. from lücke).

East Ridge (to South Summit). *A splendid climb, both long and difficult on mixed terrain, the best on the mtn. This 800m. ridge can be divided into three sections; the lower 300m. rising from the glacier, the three great towers rising to pt.2988m., and the final rock/snow/ice ridge leading the summit block, V+. First ascent: M. Betschart and F. Auf der Mauer, 1962. Diagram, p.112.*

212. From the Voralp hut ascend NW over the Wallenburfirn to pt.2536m. This marks the foot of the E ridge. Work N round foot for a short way and climb a 40m. couloir slanting L. Above the couloir, climb easy scree and rocks for 45m., then trend L for 15m. to a large projecting block on the ridge. Go up 25m., then L to a ledge. From here climb R up a crack system to reach a block-formed wall. Climb these blocks for 35m. to a good stance. Now move 20m. L to below a block and climb this round the corner on the L and go up 5m. in a dièdre to a good stance. Climb steeply for 3m., then more easily for a rope-length to a niche. Move L, then climb steep delicate rocks for 30m. to a terrace. From the middle of the terrace climb for 8m. (V), then trend L for 25m. to a large scree terrace, Climb the next steep section direct and follow a narrow ledge, below an area of red rocks, to join the ridge. The ridge now leads to a

Sustenhorn group NE

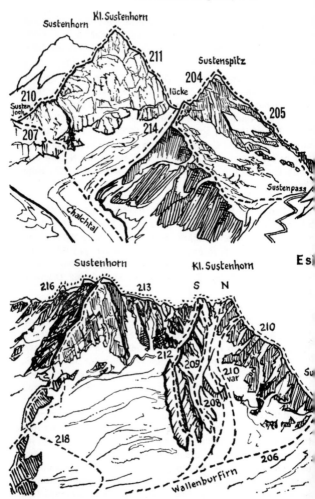

Sustenhorn · Kl. Sustenhorn

210 · 207 · Sustenjoch · 211 · lücke · 204 · Sustenspitz · 205 · 214 · Sustenpass · Chalchtal

Sustenhorn · Kl. Sustenhorn · Es

216 · 213 · S · N · 210

212 · 209 · 210 var · 208 · Su

218 · 206 · Wallenbürfirn

point above the gap before the first tower. This marks the end of the first section.

Descend a loose chimney on the N side for 15m., then climb the exposed ridge crest to the first obstacle on the tower, which is taken first R, then L, in the middle, and finally on the R to the ridge above. From the next small gap climb the slabby ridge, keeping somewhat R, up to the second tower. Move a few m. L to reach a chimney and climb this to the small gap between a gendarme and the arched tower. Avoid this tower on the N side and reach a gap in the ridge beyond. Climb the next steep pitch (V+) from R to L, then go up the exposed ridge to the top of the third tower (pt.2988m.). Now continue along the serrated ridge to a large snow saddle. End of second section.

From the saddle climb the next step directly up to the snow crest above. Follow the snow ridge and climb over rocky outcrops, taking the easiest lines according to conditions. From the last tower climb the sharp snow ridge for about 100m. to below the summit wall. Keep to the crest of the steep rocky *kante* (III), sometimes icy, and either climb the final snow slope direct or avoid it by rocks to the R (12–13h. from the hut).

Ridge Traverse from Sustenhorn (S–N). *An interesting route in itself, but a splendid mountaineering expedition if done in conjunction with an ascent of the E ridge (Route 218) to the Sustenhorn and a descent of the NE ridge (Route 210) from the Kl. Sustenhorn to the Sustenjoch; thence back to the hut.* II, *for the traverse. First traverse: R. Helbling, 4 September, 1898. Diagram, p.112.*

213. From the Sustenhorn (Route 218) climb the short rock ridge, then along an easy snow ridge to pt.3349m. Now descend a somewhat broken ridge to a deep depression, then pleasantly up a sound ridge, keeping to the crest as far as the Kl. Sustenhorn S Summit. From here descend steep rocks on the W side for a short distance, then traverse the flank to reach a couloir descending W from gap between the two summits. Ascend the couloir to this gap, then climb to the N summit by the ridge. It is also possible to keep to the crest of the ridge for the S summit, turning a large steep rock tower on the W side, or by abseiling directly from the tower to the ridge below (3–5h.).

West and North Walls. *Both these walls have routes but are loose and extremely unpleasant and are consequently omitted from the guide.*

CHALCHTALLÜCKE   2759m.

Not named on LK. The deepest gap in ridge between the Sustenspitz and Kl. Sustenhorn. It is solely used for an ascent or descent of the Kl. Sustenhorn by its NW ridge. The ridge up to the Sustenspitz is too loose and broken to be of any interest and there is no route to the lücke from the W. *Diagram, p.112.*

214. From Chalchtal—easy. Keep to the N (R) side of the Chalchtalfirn all the way up to the lücke (1½h.).

SUSTENHORN   3504m.

The highest and most southerly of the Sustenhörner. Flanked on all sides by great glaciers it gives the appearance from the W of a gentle snow peak, but to the E a series of precipitous icy cliffs rise in savage splendour above the ice. The E ridge is the best climb on the mtn; as yet no route has been made on the NE wall.

South-West Flank and South Ridge. *An easy pleasant snow climb. the normal route from the Tierbergli hut. It is also a popular ski route. The ridge from pt.3287m. can sometimes be badly corniced. I. First descent: Gottlieb Studer with Joh. and Heinrich v. Weissenfluh, 17 August, 1841.*

215. From the hut follow Route 220 to the flat névés below the Sustenlimmi. Slant NE on steepening snow to reach pt.3287m

From here follow the snow ridge to summit (cornices) ($1\frac{1}{2}$–2h.).

This route can also be followed in about the same time by taking Route 219 to the Sustenlimmi, from the Kehlenalp hut.

South Ridge (from Flachensteinfirn). *An easy climb but the glacier can be badly crevassed and the bergschrund very awkward. Useful as a descent route* I. *First ascent: Aug Naef with Joseph Zraggen, 4 August, 1889. Diagram, p.112.*

216. From the Voralp hut cross the Reuss stream and climb easy rocks N of the glacier tongue which descends E into the valley, to reach the glacier above. Traverse up in a WNW direction to a small cwm formed by two distinct rocky ribs descending from the main ridge, At the back of this cwm climb a snow couloir to the saddle, pt.3287m. Late in the season the bergschrund is sometimes impossible to cross. Now follow Route 215 up the easy snow ridge to summit ($4\frac{1}{2}$–5h. from Voralp hut).

Hinter Sustenlimmihorn (3194m.)—*Vorder Sustenlimmihorn* (3315m.)—**Sustenhorn traverse (South–North).** *An excellent climb, only moderately difficult and recommended. Neither of these two minor mtns., only marked as pts. on the LK., are of much interest alone, but this climb includes the best of the two ridges, the S and SE respectively.* II. *First descent of Hinter Sustenlimmihorn S ridge: R. Helbling and H. Pfister, 21 April, 1901 and after the first ascent of the N ridge. First ascent of Vorder Sustenlimmihorn SE ridge: O. Fischer with A. Nägeli, August, 1903.*

217. From the Kehlenalplücke (Routes 224/225) turn the first large rock tower to the SW (L) and go up a scree gully to crest of the ridge above, below the summit block. Climb the steep sharp ridge direct to top, pt.3194m., or take an easier way up a chimney on the S side.

Descend to the gap below, keeping to the steep ridge at

first, then descending on the W side (L). Now follow the sharp
and serrated ridge to summit, pt.3315m. Soon descend to a
saddle below, pt.3287m., then follow Route 215 along the S
ridge to the Sustenhorn (2–2½h. from Kehlenalplücke).

East Ridge. *A splendid climb; the best and hardest on the
Sustenhorn. III/IV; The ridge is prone to icy conditions which
can vary the difficulties considerably. First ascent: O. Fischer
and Fr. Weber, 13 July, 1901. Diagram, p.112.*

218. From the Voralp hut climb NW over the Wallenburfirn past
the rocks of pt.2653.4m. L. Now slant up L over the crevassed
Flachensteinfirn, keeping the rocks to the L, and reach a snow
gap in the E ridge, which descends into the glacier and joins
to the rocky crest of pt.2653.4m. It is also possible to climb
these rocks (not difficult) from the Wallenburfirn, thus avoiding
the crevassed glacier. From the gap climb the sharp ridge
crest, then descend to a depression before the main summit
ridge. Climb rocks somewhat on the R which lead to a small
steep snowfield. Cross this to reach crest of the ridge on the
first buttress. Follow this ridge to below the next buttress
which is climbed on N side over steep rocks, ice or snow to
the snow ridge above. Continue along the ridge, rock, snow
keeping slightly R, up to the third buttress. Take the steep
R-hand rocky edge and climb this to the upper summit ridge
which is followed at an easier angle to top (6–7h.).

SUSTENLIMMI   3091m.
An easy snow pass between the Gwächtenhorn and pt.3315m
One of the best and quickest routes from the Kehlenalp hut
in the Göschener valley to the Tierbergli hut above Stein. A
popular ski pass. I. First ascent: Gottlieb Studer with J. and
H. v. Weissenfluh, 7 August, 1841. First crossing: C. B
Hutchinson with Christian Lauener Jnr., July, 1863.

219. From Kehlenalp hut. From the hut follow the path N till
it merges into snow, then climb directly over easy névé to
pass (2h.).

220. From Tierbergli hut. From the hut go SE over easy névé to pass (crevasses in places) (1h.).

WÄCHTENHORN   3425m.

A large impressive snow peak S of the Tierbergli hut; one of the most popular climbs from the hut. From Stein or the Sustenpass this mtn. is the central dominating feature of the Sustenhörner–Tierberg cirque. Numerous easy and somewhat uninteresting routes have been omitted, and only those of immediate interest have been included. First ascent: R. W. W. Elliot Forster and L'Hardy-Dufour with Joh. v. Weissenfluh and a second guide, August, 1861.

West Ridge. *A good combination ridge climb; quite steep and exposed in places. One of the most popular routes from the Tierbergli hut. A traverse is recommended by ascending this ridge and descending the E ridge to the Sustenlimmi (Route 222).* I+. *First ascent:* W. A. B. Coolidge with Chr. Almer, Jnr., July, 1889.

221. From the Tierberglimmi (Route 187) (crevasses) follow the snow ridge to the first rocky buttress. Turn this on the L. (N) over steep snow (sometimes a bergschrund) then return to ridge. Climb the serrated ridge, keeping to the crest as much as possible, avoiding difficulties as necessary on the L. (N) over snow, up to the last rock tower. Take this direct, by the crack formed by a detached slab, or on the L. Above this follow the delicate snow ridge to summit (1½h. from pass).

East Ridge. *An easy snow climb, best used for a descent. A popular ski route.* I. *First ascensionists.*

222. From the Sustenlimmi (Route 220) climb broad, easy-angled névé, finally up a short snow ridge to summit (1h. from pass).

South-South-West Ridge. *The best and the most difficult route from the Kehlenalp hut.* IV.

223. From the Kehlenalp hut climb the Kehlen glacier. Go up to pt.2778m. which marks the foot of the ridge. Start E of this pt.

beside a large scree cone with a gully above. Climb the steep W side of the gully for one rope-length (IV), then slant L up a wide ramp. Above, climb a groove and continue up the next ridge for several rope-lengths to below a pyramidal buttress. Climb this L for two-thirds its height, then traverse R across an easy ledge (invisible from below) to the R edge of the buttress which is climbed direct; steep and delicate (IV). After this follow the ridge more easily to and over a 40m. buttress which is taken direct. Climb the next tower direct on good holds (pegs), but turn the upper pinnacle to the R to reach the ridge beyond. On this ridge traverse a number of gendarmes to another large tower. Abseil R down a gully, then climb for two rope-lengths. Bear R to reach the ridge which is followed to the S summit, 3375.2m. From here continue along the easy ridge to main summit (4–5h. from foot of climb).

KEHLENALPLÜCKE   3092m.

Not marked on LK.:50,000. An easy and popular pass between the Voralp and Kehlenalp huts. Care should be taken on account of crevasses on Voralp side. I.

224. From Voralp hut. From the hut follow Route 216 to the Flachensteinfirn. Cross the glacier W to the pass; the deepest gap in ridge between the Brunnenstock, 3210.6m. (L) and the Hinter Sustenlimmihorn, 3194m. (R). The pass is easily recognised between two prominent rock towers. Climb a wide couloir to top (2–3h.).

225. From Kehlenalp hut. From the hut go N and follow a clear track along a prominent rib running up through the snow. Continue up this track till it bears R on to the glacier, then cross E over easy névé (no crevasses) to pass. Climb a short easy couloir to top (2–2½h.).

BRUNNENSTOCK 3210.6m.

A small but attractive rock peak lying immediately S of the Kehlenalplücke. Unfortunately the rock is poor and consequently the mtn. is infrequently climbed except in winter when it becomes a very popular ski route from the Kehlenalp hut. The SW ridge is the best climb, the SE being too loose to be enjoyable. I/II. First ascent: C. Seelig and J. Veitl, 30 August, 1891. First winter ascent: F. Comtesse and W. Muggli and Heinrich Däniker, 1 April, 1937.

226. From the Kehlenalp hut follow Route 225 nearly to the foot of the Kehlenalplücke. Move R and climb a gully to the SW ridge, which is followed without difficulty to summit (3h. from hut).

VORALPHORN 3203m.

A minor peak of no great importance or interest, S of the Brunnenstock. Easily climbed from the Voralp hut over the Flachensteinfirn. A couloir leads to the S ridge which is followed to summit. The bergschrund can sometimes be difficult. First ascent: Oscar Schuster with P. Gamma and a porter, 25 July, 1897.

KEHLENALPHORN 3196m.

The rock peak immediately S of the Voralphorn. A small mtn. not named on LK.; nevertheless the rock is good and there are two interesting climbs.

South-East Ridge. *A good route, all too short.* II+. *First ascent: W. A. Keller and Jean Munck, June, 1910.*

227. From the Horefellilücke (Routes 229/230) climb the S-facing wall by a series of slabs, short chimneys and ledges to the ridge. On the ridge climb a steep red tower, then follow a level ridge to summit (1–2h. from lücke).

South Ridge. *A steep impressive ridge descending to the upper Hinter Mur NE from the Kehlenalp hut. A feature of the ridge is a*

large projecting buttress separated at the foot of the true S ridge
by a deep gap, pt.2889m. The presence of the lower buttress
creates two distinct routes; the S ridge normal (IV) and the
buttress route (V/V+). Both are good climbs and a combination
of the two affords a splendid climb. First ascent of the S ridge
normal: brothers Jost and Paul Mattli, August, 1960. First ascent
of buttress variation: Willy Auf der Maur, Alois Lüönd and Franz
Auf der Maur, 25, June, 1961.

228. From the Kehlenalp hut follow Route 219 towards the
Sustenlimmi pass, as far as the 2800m. contour. Traverse
R (E) across snow, and keep on this all the way up to the foot of
the buttress. The climb starts a little round to the SE (R).
Climb for one rope length over easy rocks to a niche (peg
stance). Climb directly for 15m. to a poor stance R of an overhang. Climb L over smooth slabs to a crack and go up this
delicately for 20m. to a wide terrace (V+, pegs and wedges).
Traverse R to the ridge and climb this to the top of the buttress
(V−). Abseil 40m. to the gap below at the foot of the true S
ridge. (1½–2h.). (It is now possible to abandon the climb by
descending W or E). From the gap follow the remainder of
the S ridge pleasantly to summit (4h, from gap).

HOREFELLILÜCKE   3021m.

A pass between the Kehlenalphorn (3196m.) and the N. Hoch
Horefellistock (3175m.). Not named on LK. It affords a fairly
quick and easy route between the Kehlenalp and Voralp
huts. I. First crossing: Oscar Schuster with P. Gamma, 20
November, 1897.

229. From the SW. From the Kehlenalp hut follow Route 228
to the foot of the Kehlenalphorn S buttress. Continue E a
short way then climb L into a small snow-filled cwm. Climb
a steep obvious gully to the pass (1½–2h.).

230. From the NE. From the Voralp hut follow Route 216 to the
Flachensteinfirn, then bear SW across the glacier (a few
crevasses) to the obvious pass (1½–2h.).

HOCH HOREFELLISTOCK   S. Summit, 3176m.,
N. Summit, 3175m.

A relatively unimportant mtn. SE of the Horefellilücke. The
S ridge is the only recommended route; other climbs are
tedious and uninteresting.

South Ridge. *This is the best climb, but details are somewhat
vague and little is known of it.* IV.

231. From the Kehlenalp or Bergsee huts follow Route 232
to the couloir of the normal route. Climb this as far as the first
steep rocks, then traverse out L across a scree covered terrace
to reach the S ridge, which is recognised by a distinct rock
needle. This is turned by descending slightly on the E side, then
climb the steep ridge to summit (1½–2h. from start).

South Flank and South-East Ridge (to S Summit). *The
normal route, easy with no great interest. It is best used for
descent after the S ridge.* I. *First ascent: Oscar Schuster and
Jos Gamma, 20 November, 1897.*

232. From the Bergsee hut climb NW through Vorder Mur
to pt.2669m. This pt. can also be reached from the Kehlenalp
hut by following Route 228 to the foot of the Kehlenalphorn
S ridge, then descending SE. Ascend a little further round
NW, to reach a couloir descending from the ridge between
pt.3176m. and the Schijenstock, 3161.2m. Climb this couloir
on the R (S) side to the ridge above. Now traverse up and
out on to the SW side of the SE ridge, and climb to the S summit,
pt.3176m. The N summit is easily reached by following the
connecting ridge. As the rocks are easy, other variations
exist on the S flank; one is to climb from the couloir direct up
to the summit without bothering with the ridge (1½–2h.).

SCHIJENSTOCK   3161.2m.

The immediate SE neighbour of the Hoch Horefellistock;
a much more interesting mtn. with some first-class climbs.

South Ridge. *A splendid ridge and an excellent climb on good rock. The lower part takes the form of a steep buttress followed by a series of jagged towers, which soon steepen into a buttress rising to the summit wall. 400m. IV. First ascent: O. Gerecht, F. Wörndle and A. E. Meier, 22 August, 1948.*

233. From the Bergsee hut go NNW over scree, grass and easy rocks to foot of the ridge, pt.2765m. Follow the steep ridge, climbing over 10 rock towers, keeping as close as possible to the crest, to summit. It is necessary to abseil from three of the towers to continue on the ridge (4½–5h. from start).

South-East Wall. *A fine climb on perfect rock. 300m. V. First ascent: Bruno Boller and Alois Regli, 11 September, 1949.*

234. From the Bergsee hut ascend N to the large level cwm of the Schijenstock—Bergseeschijen. Go up a scree cone at the back (L) then diagonally up a snow couloir to its top R-hand side, to reach the centre of the wall. This couloir leads up L towards the S ridge. It can be easier to keep on snow R of the scree cone to reach the couloir, thus avoiding a somewhat unpleasant scramble over scree.

Climb L, at first without difficulty, then go up R steeply for at least three rope lengths to below a prominent block overhang. Traverse R then climb direct on steep delicate rock for several rope lengths to below a second roof. Climb this roof with direct aid from pegs, then slant up for 3m. Now climb direct to a third overhang. Do not climb the wide crack to its R, which is full of loose dangerous blocks; traverse horizontally 4m. R then climb a thin crack which slants R. Continue slanting R to the yellow upper part of the wall, then move further R to reach the exit crack, which leads L to summit (5½–6h. from hut).

Descent by East Ridge.

235. From the summit descend E ridge, keeping to the easy angled L (NE) side, to the deepest gap before it rises to the Bergseeschijen. Descend a couloir on the R (SW) side to the cwm above Bergsee hut (1–2h.).

BERGSEESCHIJEN 2815.5m.

One of the most important and frequented mtns. in the Sustenhorn group, especially after the building of the Bergsee hut. A good selection of excellent climbs on perfect rock between grades IV and VI, one of the classic being the S ridge. On all other routes a variety of wedges and pegs should be taken. Opportunities still exist for new routes and variations. Together with the Feldschijen and Salbitschijen, probably the most attractive climbing in Central Switzerland for the British rock climbing purist.

South Ridge. *A very good climb, steep and exposed; one of the most popular on the mtn. 300m. IV. First ascent: Bruno Boller and Alois Regli, 28 September, 1949. Diagram, p.126.*

236. The ridge is easily recognised by a conspicuous smooth slab at its foot with a great rocky bastion to the immediate S. From the Bergsee hut slant up NE to foot of the climb. Avoid the bastion (L) and reach a gap between it and the start of the true ridge; the smooth slab. Go up R for 5m. then climb delicately for 20m. to a ledge above. A little L then R, then climb a series of thin cracks for 2 or 3 rope lengths to reach a grassy stance. Climb direct over steep difficult rocks for three rope lengths to reach the ridge above. Follow this more easily and pleasantly to summit (4–5h. from hut).

South Wall (Var. I). *A steep interesting climb on good rock. IV/V —. First ascent: Röbi Zwinggi and Franz Anderrüthi, 23 September, 1961.*

237. From the Bergsee hut follow Route 236 to the gap behind the bastion of the S ridge. Traverse R easily for 30m. then climb a groove for 10m. to a belaying spike. Climb steeply in an open dièdre (2 pegs) to a tiny stance (pegs). Continue up a dièdre (pegs), then 20m. L to a stance on a rocky rib (one peg). Follow this rib, then move R to a stance (pegs). Trend a little L, then climb R to a peg stance. Climb direct over slabs (pegs), then R to a stance (pegs). Continue up slabs (pegs) and a dièdre (R) which leads to the S ridge. Follow this to summit (4–5h. from hut).

South Wall (Var. II). *Another good climb on the S wall, close to Route 237, of similar length but somewhat more difficult.* V.
238. From the gap behind the bastion traverse R for 20m. along an easy ledge. Then climb direct for 5m. to a peg, then up L for a further 8m. to a vague traversing crack (pegs). Follow this crack up L for approx. 15m. to a small stance (pegs). A little L, then climb thin cracks (pegs) for 12m. to a wide ledge; stance. Climb a steep, open and somewhat grassy crack for 20m., then traverse R for about 15m. along a narrow ledge to a stance (pegs). Trend R across slabs to a rib and follow this for 12m. to a stance (pegs). Climb directly up the steep edge for 20m., then up a dièdre (pegs) (L) for 15m. to a stance. Go up L of the edge for 40m., climbing a series of cracked slabs (pegs) to a stance. A short traverse R, then climb a dièdre and a slab above it to join the S ridge which is followed to summit (4–5h. from hut).

South-East Pillar. *A good climb, similar in length and difficulty to those on S wall.* V, A2. First ascent: F. Anderrüthi and K. Grüter, 1960.
239. The climb starts below and to the R of Var. II of the S wall. Traverse easily further R down from this route, and start R of a distinct cwm edge which merges higher up into the E wall. Climb a small dièdre (V, A2) to a small block. Slant up 4m. R to below a small roof (V). Climb this R and continue to a stance R (pegs). Work up easy rocks R to the pillar. Take a small dièdre, then climb a slabby wall above (V) to a good stance. Now climb the next ridge, first on R then on L side. Finally climb a short, steep slab (V) to a platform. At this point the climb joins the S ridge which is followed to summit (4–5h. from hut).

East Wall. *A splendid route; very difficult, exposed and sustained, though with some excellent stances.* 350m., VI, A3. First ascent: Hugo Borer, Werner Wymann and Helmut Walther, 8/9 February, 1967. Diagram, p.126.

240. In the centre of the wall there is a series of prominent roofs; the climb starts in a line leading to the R side of these. From the Bergsee hut go up below the S ridge and up into the cwm below the E wall. Climb directly on good holds to a crack, which is followed for 30m. (V+, pegs), then a short, steep step L to a large stance. Continue direct in a strenuous overhanging chimney (wedges) to a good stance. Go L then climb a dièdre to below a large roof (VI, pegs). Climb the overhang L and go up to a small stance below a roof (peg stance). A short traverse L then climb an overhanging dièdre which merges into a smooth wall below an overhang. Slant R up a very smooth slab to below a roof (A2, étrier stance). Climb R to below the great barrier of roofs which project for about 20m. from the wall. Traverse L on to the wall below the roofs (A3, pegs and wedges) to reach a small stance (pegs). Climb a crack for 40m. to a good stance, and continue for two rope lengths to a large stance. A further two rope lengths in the same direction lead to a good belay. Now make a short traverse L and climb L to a smooth slab. Climb moving R (delicate) to another good stance. A steep crack (pegs) leads to a small belay behind a spike. Climb smooth slabby rocks to below a roof (VI−, pegs), then traverse R delicately for 40m. to a tiny stance (pegs). Take the next smooth dièdre which leads to the E ridge a short distance from summit (10–12h. from the hut).

East Wall Pillar. *A recent climb, not quite as difficult as the E wall route but equally interesting. 300m., V+, A2. First ascent: Hugo Borer, Werner Wymann and Helmut Walther, 4 June, 1967. Diagram, p.126.*

241. Start 10m. R of the E wall route (240). Climb for 15m. on good holds to a corner crack which is followed for 20m. A further 25m. direct then make a 2m. traverse R. Climb a crack for 10m. to a good stance. Go 4m. L to the pillar edge, then climb for 25m. to an étrier stance. Climb direct for 5m., make a rising traverse L for 5m., then go up smooth slabs to below a roof. Turn this on the L then climb a yellow dièdre for 15m.

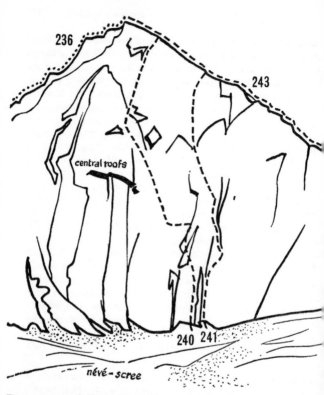

Bergseeschijen E wall

to a stance. Now L for 10m. to the pillar edge and follow this for several rope lengths to top of the pillar. Finally one rope length R leads to the E ridge and climb this to summit (11h. for first ascent).

West Wall. *A very hard and predominantly free climb. Very little real information as to the quality and other aspects is known; a generous time allowance should be made. The present editor experienced some difficulty finding the start of the climb shortly after the first ascent, and what he found he did not like. This is not conclusive, as a retreat was called for before the climb had really begun. 250m., VI, A1. First ascent: Sepp Inwyler and B. Krauthahn, 1958.*

242. As for Route 236 to the bastion below the S ridge. Continue up L past the bastion to below the W wall. The wall is cut by a distinct dièdre; the climb starts in a line L of this feature. Climb a small rib and somewhat grassy rocks to a stance. Bear L up a steep slab to a belay. Climb more delicate slabs then traverse L to a rocky belaying spike (V). Descend a little and cross to two ribs and a crack which is climbed to a small stance. Climb an overhanging dièdre above (VI−), then traverse L to a stance. Continue R to a small overhang. Climb this then continue steeply for 20m. (VI−) to an awkward sloping stance. Climb L to an overhang (poor rock) which is taken on the R, tiny stance. Up a few m. steeply then bear L to a small stance (VI). Climb difficult rock above for a rope length to a belay (VI). Climb the next dièdre, traverse L, then continue up overhanging rock to a stance (VI). A small overhang above is followed by a dièdre which leads to another overhang. Climb this direct (A1) to a stance. Take the next dièdre and climb this till a few m. below a large jammed block. Now go on to the overhanging R wall and climb this to a stance. An overhanging dièdre above, (A1, then free, VI) leads finally to easier rock. Trend R to the summit ridge, about 40m. from top (8h. for first ascent).

East Ridge. *An easy ridge; the normal descent route. I. First ascent: H. and A. Müller, 19 August, 1931. Diagram, p.126.*

243. From the Bergsee hut go NE then N to the Bergseeschijen-Hochschijen cwm. Climb to the deepest gap in the connecting ridge of these two mtns., then follow the broad easy ridge to summit (1½–2h. from hut).

North-West Ridge. *Another easy descent route which joins Route 235; the normal descent from the Schijenstock.*

HOCHSCHIJEN   2634m.

A small rock peak immediately E of the Bergseeschijen. To date only one route seems to have been recorded.

South Ridge. *This would appear to be a fairly good and interesting climb, but no detail seems to be available as to the grade, first ascent or other relevant information.*

244. From the Bergsee hut climb NE to reach the foot of the S ridge. This is easily recognised. Climb an obvious dièdre for two rope lengths on its slabby R-hand side. Traverse approx. 10m. L along a narrow ledge, then climb steep cracks to the L edge. Follow this to a small stance. Go R to the ridge and climb this to the first rock tower. Turn this on its N side over loose rock to reach the gap beyond. Climb the second steep tower direct, and continue over several rocky teeth to the summit block, which is turned on the L by a dièdre (4h. from hut).

Descent. *Descend the easy W ridge to the deepest gap in the connecting ridge of the Hochschijen–Bergseeschijen, to join the normal descent route of the latter mtn. (Route 243).*

GRANDSCHIJEN   2388.3m.

The last and most easterly mtn. in this group. Easily ascended on the N (Voralp) side, but to the S you find a series of steep, difficult, granite walls. Not quite as popular as its westerly neighbours, as it has to be climbed from the road and not the Bergsee hut. A good selection of pegs and wedges should be taken on both routes.

South Wall Dièdre. *An excellent route on good rock; a mixture of free and artificial climbing. 220m., V+, A2. 16 wooden wedges and 15 pegs used on first ascent: Freddy Rebmann and Heinz Bächli, 1 August, 1964 (8h.) Second ascent: Walther Stähli and Erich Friedli, in 5h.*

245. From Gwüest, a small village on the road up to the Göscheneralpsee, follow the path to Börtli, 1803m., then up past pt.1929m. to foot of the wall. A very large dièdre cuts the wall; the first rope length takes a line R of this. Start the climb 6 to 8m. R (E) of the foot of a pillar which is formed by the R edge of the dièdre. Climb direct for 40m. (A1) to a good stance, then traverse L to a stance in the dièdre. Go up L past two roofs (A2) and from there climb straight up (A1) to a small stance. Traverse L out to the edge and up 6m. to a good stance. Now climb up a short steep step to a dièdre and go up this for 8/10m. to a narrow ledge which is followed L out to a pillar. Climb directly up this (A1) to a small fir tree, then trend R and cross a smooth slab, up to a stance.

Follow a grassy ledge L to a niche, then climb R up a slabby wall to a second grassy ledge, which ends in a niche; stance. Turn the great slab above R (A2), then traverse L, up along its upper edge, to a good stance on a grassy ledge. Climb the L wall of the next chimney-like dièdre for 40m., and exit L on to a narrow ledge. Now traverse slightly L along a ledge to the edge, and climb this; then move L to a stance. Take the slab above direct (A1) and finally climb easier steps to summit (5–6h. from start. It takes approx. 1½h. to reach the foot of the wall from Gwüest).

South Wall. *The first route to be done on this wall. A good short hard climb with far more free moves than the S wall dièdre. 260m., V+/VI−. First ascent: Hermann Kaufmann and Freddy Rebmann, 6 July, 1963.*

246. Start about 35m. E (R) of the great dièdre (245). Climb direct, then trend L up the slabby wall to a narrow ledge; stance to R. Traverse L in a crack for 15 m. to a chimney; stance.

Now climb direct, then exit R using a prominent crack and
climb the wall for two rope lengths to a stance beside a detached
flake. Climb direct up the gap behind the flake to a stance in a
niche. Go up to below a small roof, traverse R to a grassy
ledge and climb 6m. to a good stance. The upper wall is climbed
by a dièdre on the R; finally go up easy grassy rocks to summit
($3\frac{1}{2}$–4h. from foot of wall).

Descent.

247. The quickest and best route is to descend the easy E
ridge to pt.2251m., then go down SW back to foot of the wall.

PART V

FLECKISTOCK GROUP

The most easterly range in the area covered by this guide. A compact group forming a high mtn. ridge running NW–SE, with the most important peaks, Stucklistock, Fleckistock, Winterberg and Rorspitzli lying to the immediate E of the Voralp hut. These mtns. must rank among the most impressive and beautiful of the Central Swiss Alps. From the W they appear in savage rocky splendour above the Voralptal and surrounding glaciers. To the NE steep walls of rock and ice rise precipitously from the green Meiental, giving an air of inaccessibility and great height. With the modern pre-dominant trend towards extreme climbing the area has been somewhat neglected. With the exception of a few routes on the Wildauenenhöreli and Meiggelenstock, none of the climbs are difficult, but there is an excellent selection of high ridge routes and traverses on good rock; all within easy access of the Voralp and Salbit huts.

Several good climbs are to be had above Dörfli and Wassen near the beginning of the Susten pass, but to date these have been the preserve of the local enthusiast, being within easy climbing distance. The lack of hut accommodation and the lengthy approaches are a deterrent to many. For those who appreciate and enjoy a long walk with a good climb at the end, in a wild and unspoilt mtn. area, this would not apply.

KLEIN GRIESSENHORN 2851m.

A minor peak, the most northerly in the Fleckistock group. All the routes are easy; the most interesting climb is the traverse of the NW and N ridge to the Gross Griessenhorn and Stucklistock.

Klein Griessenhorn–Stucklistock traverse. *A good interesting ridge climb, nowhere exceeding II.*

247. Reach the Griessen Alp, pt.1951m., either from Färnigen via a path leading NW or from the road by going due S from pt.1739m. From the Alp go in WSW direction to foot of the NW ridge. Follow the crest of the ridge over the top and descend to the saddle at pt.2889m. Now join Route 253 and continue along the ridge over the Gross Griessenhorn to the Stucklistock (5–6h.).

East Flank. *An easy, quick route; pleasant for descent.* I/II
248. From the Griessen Alp, pt.1951m. (247) go SW and ascend the Griessen névé. Climb a distinct snow couloir which leads to a gap in the SE ridge. From this gap soon climb the ridge to top. In a very dry season the top of this couloir can be of slabby rock, not snow (2–3h.).

GROSS GRIESSENHORN   3202m.

The southerly neighbour of the Klein. Of no great importance and usually only climbed in conjunction with Routes 247/253.

STUCKLISTOCK   3308.4m.

A steep impressive rock peak with a variety of interesting routes, none of which are very difficult or long. The classic climb is traversing from the Stucklistock to the Fleckistock.

South Wall and South-East Ridge. *A fairly easy route, useful for descending.* II. *First ascent: Ed Hoffmann and F. Hoffmann-Merian with J. M. Tresch, Ambros and Hans Zgraggen, 28 August, 1865. Diagram, p.135.*
249. From the Voralp hut follow Route 206 on to the Wallen-burfirn, then slant up NE over a large scree cone to reach a terrace running between pts.2667m. and 2571.9m. Now cross the Hangfirn in a northerly direction towards a snow couloir rising to a saddle SE of the Stucklistock. Climb this couloir, keeping on the N (L) side for about half height, then move up L on fairly good rock to join the SE ridge just below summit (3–4h. from hut).

South-East Ridge. *An interesting route, one of the best climbs on the mtn.* III. *First descent: E. Huber and C. Seelig with J. Zgraggen, 17 November, 1889. Diagram, p.135.*

250. From the Voralp hut follow Route 249 to the snow couloir. Climb this to the saddle, then follow the ridge directly to summit (4–5h. from hut).

South-West Ridge. *An easy, interesting climb.* II. *First ascent: W. C. Compton, A. V. Valentine-Richards with Abr. Müller and Siegfried Burgener, 23 August, 1899. Diagram, p.135.*

251. From the Voralp hut follow Route 249 to the Hangfirn. Go NW to a snow couloir which rises to the ridge, which is then followed to summit (4½–5h. from hut).

South-West Rib. *An excellent steep route on good rock.* III. *First ascent: A. Pfister, Rudi Martin, M. Waber, H. Ritter and E. Marti, 31 May, 1903. Diagram, p.135.*

252. From the Voralp hut follow Route 249 to the Hangfirn. Cross to the SW wall and go to the foot of a well-defined steep rock rib. Climb this rib on its crest to the W ridge above; the most difficult section is at mid-height (3h. from foot of rib).

North Ridge. *A pleasant climb,* II. *First ascent: Carl Egger and Franz von Salis, 26 July, 1903.*

253. From the Voralp hut follow Route 206 to the Sustenjoch and reach the small glacier NW of the Stucklistock. Climb to the saddle between the Klein Griessenhorn and Stucklistock, pt.2889m.; then follow the ridge over the Gross Griessenhorn to the Stucklistock (3h. from saddle).

South-West Chimney. *Quite a steep hard route.* III. *First ascent: Emil Meier and Arthur Baumgarner, 22 September, 1943. Diagram, p.135.*

254. From the Hangfirn (Route 249) cross to the foot of the S wall, L of the SW rib (Route 252). Ascend a steep couloir to reach an obvious chimney which rises towards the W ridge above. Climb this chimney, avoiding the most difficult section by going on the L wall. Finally climb the steep chimney, then over easier rocks to the W ridge just below summit (5½–6h. from hut).

Stucklistock–Fleckistock Traverse. *Undoubtedly the finest climb to be done from the Voralp hut. Nowhere very difficult but fairly long, on good rock and in a perfect situation. III. First traverse S to N: H. Frick with J. M. Gamma, 15 July, 1900. Diagram, p.135.*

255. From the Voralp hut follow Route 253 to summit of the Stucklistock and descend the SE ridge (250) to saddle. From here follow the crest of the main ridge, past pt.3317m., to below the NW ridge of the Fleckistock. Now follow this steeply to the summit and descend the SSE ridge to the N. Flüelücke (258) (for the circuit, hut to hut, 8–10h.).

FLECKISTOCK or ROT STOCK   3416.5m.

A fine peak, one of the most impressive mtns. in this group. The rock is generally good and most of the climbs from the Voralp side are interesting; the classic being the Stucklistock-Fleckistock traverse. There are several routes on the N and NE sides but these have not been included. None can be recommended, and all take at least 5–6h. over difficult terrain from the valley to reach the foot of the climbs; or a lengthy, complicated glacier approached from the Flühlücke. There is no hut on this side. First ascent: A. Raillard and L. Fininger with Ambros Zgraggen and Kasper Blatter, 21 July, 1864.

South-West Rib and South-South-East Ridge. *A good interesting rock ridge, nowhere difficult. II. First ascent: C. Seelig with J. Zgraggen, 21 October, 1888. Diagram, p.135.*

256. From the Voralp hut go up E to Flüestafel, just above pt.2385m. The secondary summit pt.3251m. is directly above to the N. Climb N into the cwm; when level with a gap in the secondary ridge which rises from pt.2553.3m., traverse L to

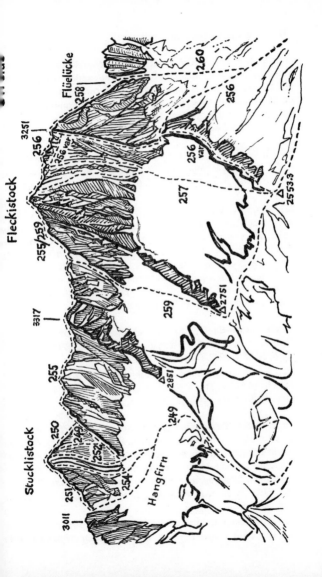

join the foot of the SW rib. It is also possible to reach this point by following the crest of this secondary ridge from pt.2553.3m. Climb this rib to the summit, pt.3251m. From here continue along the upper S ridge and finally along the SE ridge, turning a large rock tower on its S side, to the main summit (4–5h. from hut).

South-West Flank. *An easy route of no special merit, but useful for descending.* I/II. *First ascent: A. Raillard and L. Fininger with A. Zgraggen and K. Blatter, 21 July, 1864. Diagram, p.135.*

257. From the Voralp hut follow Route 256 to the foot of the SW rib at pt.2553.3m. Now slant up NE on the other side over scree and snowy rocks to foot of the wall directly below the S ridge between pts.3251m. and 3416.5m. Here is a distinct rock rib with two couloirs L and R of it, running up to the ridge. Either follow the R-hand gully to the S ridge to join Route 256, or take the rocky L edge of the L gully and climb this to just below the summit (3½–4h. from hut).

South-South-East Ridge. *An excellent climb on good rock.* II/III. *First ascent: A. Pfister, Rud. Martin, M. Wäber and E. Marti, 30 May, 1902. Diagram, p.135.*

258. From the N Flüelücke (Route 260) follow the steep SE ridge to pt.3251m., then go along the S ridge (256) to the main summit (2h. from saddle).

North-West Ridge. *One of the best climbs on the mtn.; a classic route if combined with the traverse from the Stucklistock (see Route 255). The route described here joins this climb at the saddle SE of pt.3317m., just before the steep upthrust of the NW ridge.* II/III. *First descent: E. Labhardt and R. Helbling, 26 July, 1898. First traverse: H. Frick with J. M. Gamma, 15 July, 1900. Diagram, p.135.*

259. From the Voralp hut follow Route 257, past pt.2553.3m. into the cwm below the SW wall. Continue W below and round the rocky rib at pt.2751m. Now climb NE over névé and finally up a couloir to the saddle. From here follow Route 255 to summit (1½–2h. to saddle).

FLÜELÜCKE or N FLÜHLÜCKE   2965m.

The deepest gap in the connecting ridge between the Fleckistock and Winterberg, forming an easy natural pass between the Voralp and Meien valleys. It is a popular ski pass with an exceptionally good run down to Dörfli. First crossing: R. Helbling and E. Labhardt, 18 February, 1896. *Diagram, p.135.*

260. From the West. From the Voralp hut follow Route 256 up to Flüestafel, then directly N to the pass, up a snow scree couloir. The saddle is easily recognised as the deep gap immediately below the Fleckistock SE ridge (2½–3h. from hut).

261. From the East. From Dörfli cross the stream of the Meienreuss by the small hamlet of Litzigen. Now follow a path SW via Stäfeli into the large Kartigel cwm. Continue up by pt.2312m. and cross on to the Kartigelfirn. Ascend the glacier WSW to the pass, easily recognised as the snowy saddle at the foot of the SE ridge. Bad crevasses near the foot of the rib which descends ESE from the Fleckistock (5–6h. from Dörfli).

LITZIGSTOCK   2532m.

FEDISTOCK   2767m.

Pt.2840m.

An interesting wish-bone-shaped rock ridge with three main summits. A good worthwhile climb from Dörfli is to traverse all three tops. II/III. First ascent: J. Giacometti and A. Weber, 13 February, 1904.

262. From Dörfli follow Route 261 to pt.1479.3m. just below Stäfeli. Go up NW over steep grass and rocks at first, then N up to the foot of the Litzigstock E ridge. Follow the ridge to the summit, then continue along the crest SW and S to pt.2767m. It is now possible to traverse the ridge WSW to pt.2840m., but it is necessary to return again to the same pt. From pt.2767m. climb the ridge ESE over three rock towers to below the summit block, which is climbed by a chimney on N side. Descend the ridge E to pt.1813m., thence back to Dörfli (for the round circuit 6–8h.).

WINTERBERG　3167m.

CHÜEPLANGGENSTOCK　3207.7m.

In reality one mtn. but with two separate summit names. In some references it is known as the Winterberg, in others by its somewhat longer appellation. An interesting mtn. within easy reach of the Voralp hut, but not so popular as the Fleckistock and Stucklistock.

South-West Wall. *An easy route, useful for descent.* I/II. *First ascent: R. Elmer, solo, 13 August, 1864.*

263. From the Voralp hut follow the path to Flüestafel. Traverse downwards SE then up N to reach the foot of the SW rib. Climb on the crest of this rib which rises on the wall, without difficulty, to the summit ridge which is soon followed to top ($3\frac{1}{2}$–4h. from hut).

South-West Rib. *A good route, one of the best on the mtn.* III. *First ascent: Hannes Huss and Trudi Voegeli, 20 October, 1946.*

264. From Flüestafel (Route 256) go up NE and take the first of two distinct narrow and steep rock ribs, Climb the sharp crest, surmounting two small rock towers to join the NW ridge which is followed to summit (4h. from hut).

North-West Ridge. *A fine climb which can be done in conjunction with a traverse from the Fleckistock.* III. *First ascent: V. de. Beauclair and Oscar Schuster, 14 June, 1896.*

265. From the Voralp hut follow Route 260 to below the couloir rising to the N Flühlücke. Go R (S) and climb the snow couloir to the S Flühlücke. Now climb the ridge to reach a large rock tower which is taken direct. Above the tower continue along crest of the ridge to summit (4½–5h. from hut).

North-East Wall. *A good route, steep and fairly difficult: not often done. Can be approached from Dörfli, but the best and shortest way is from the Voralp hut over the N or S Flühlücke. III/IV, some danger of stonefall. First descent: Paul Schucan and Hans Hössli, 7 June, 1903.*

266. From the Kartigelfirn (Routes 261/260) go to the foot of an obvious snow gully which descends E from the summit. Ascend this gully and climb the steep rock wall above, bearing L (S) to an obvious subsidiary ridge which is followed till you are about 100m. below the summit. Now traverse R (N) across steep slabs to immediately below the summit, then climb directly up the wall above to top (5–7h. from hut).

RORSPITZLI (KUHPLANKENSTOCK) 3220m.

An impressive mtn. with a 400m. rock wall when viewed from the Voralp valley, but with a more gentle snowy appearance from the NE. None of the climbing is difficult but the ridges are interesting and worthwhile.

South-West Flank. *An easy route of no special merit other than for descent.* I/II. *First descent: W. Gröbli with Jos. M. Gamma, 3 August, 1891.*

267. From Flüestafel above the Voralp hut traverse down SE to the foot of the SW ridge which descends from pt.3193m. Now climb a wide snow gully to the gap in the ridge between pt.3195m. and the summit; then go up the ridge to top; or climb direct to the top from the gully itself (3–5h. from hut).

North-West Ridge. *A splendid route, especially when done as a complete traverse from the Fleckistock, taking in the Winterberg. II/III, depending on choice of route combinations. First ascent: F. Grob and J. Zgraggen, 30 July, 1902.*

268. From the Winterberg follow the ridge, keeping somewhat on the L side (NE) along a series of narrow ledges, or follow the ridge crest with more difficulty to summit (1½–2h. from Winterberg).

South-East Ridge. *An excellent climb, undoubtedly the most interesting on the mtn. Nowhere very difficult but tricky to find the correct route in bad weather. The best descent routes to the Salbit hut are on the NE ridge (Route 270) and the E wall (Route 271). II/III. First ascent: Aldo Bonacossa, Carlo Prochownik and Umberto Canziani, 17 June, 1912.*

269. From the Salbit hut climb NW through Wissgand and climb the large snow couloir leading to the small Salbit glacier. Cross this (easy, no crevasses) to reach the deepest gap in the ridge (SE) between the Salbitschijen (2981.4m.) and pt.3060m. Now climb over five rock towers, the first being easy. From the top of the fourth climb down for a rope length on the Voralp side, then abseil for about 6m. to a gap in the ridge below. The very impressive fifth tower is not really difficult and is climbed direct on excellent rock. Now follow the ridge, occasionally going on to the E side up to summit (5–6h. from hut).

North-East Ridge. *Only really useful as a descent. I/II.*

270. From the Salbit glacier (Route 269) go N to a small unnamed gap in the ridge descending from pt. 3060m. at c.2940m., and cross this to the Rorfirn. Now go NE across snow (a few crevasses) to a saddle between the Rorspitzli and Spitzli, pt.3011.3m. From here follow NE ridge easily to top (4–5h.).

SPITZLI   3011.3m.

272. A somewhat unfrequented rocky mtn. lying NE of the Rorspitzli. A good route is the N ridge from pt.2311m. below the Kartigelfirn (Route 261), then a descent by the SW ridge to the saddle between the Rorspitzli and Spitzli. From here down the NW side of the Kartigelfirn to rejoin Route 261. II/III.

SCHWARZ STOCK   2635.2m.

The north-easterly neighbour of the Spitzli with three ridges running NE to pt.2209m.; ENE to the Mittagstock, 2506m, and E to Höreli 2365m. A combination of any of these three ridges from Dörfli or Wassen with a traverse to the Spitzli affords a spendid ridge tour. I/II (3–5h.).

WILDLAUENENHORELI   c.2546m.

Not marked on LK., and cannot warrant the appellation of mtn., being merely a pt. on the ridge between pts.2363m. and 2639m., E of the Schwarz Stock. To date two routes exist; both are fairly short but require quite a strenuous pull up (1288m.) from Wassen. One could camp at the little lake, pt.2204m. at the foot of the climbs but this seems an unjustifiably long way to carry heavy gear.

South-West Edge. *A fairly good climb, not sustained.* IV. *About 300m.*

273. From Wassen or Meiggelen just to the S, follow the path leading SW to pt.1026m., then W to Rorstäfeli past pt.1343m. Continue along the track N to Auf den Hüblen, then up NNE over difficult terrain to the Kl. See (little lake) at pt.2204m. From the Kl. See climb NE to foot of the *kante* which lies to the R of a wide couloir. Climb the couloir for about 20m. to reach a grassy ledge which runs out on to the *kante*. From the ledge climb a sort of groove about 15m. R of the *kante*, to reach a grassy ledge. Follow this ledge round the *kante* and climb a short dièdre on the L side which leads to the *kante* edge. Continue upwards, then a horizontal ridge-like section leads to a distinct light-coloured slab. Climb this direct for 15m. (pegs) to a large grassy area, where the *kante* merges into the W wall. Climb a short, steep wall, then up a groove (R) which leads to a small saddle beneath the summit dièdres. Climb the first two dièdres for about 30m., but leave the last dièdre after 15m. to the R, where it begins to overhang, and make a difficult, exposed traverse R across a cracked slab to reach easier rock. From here continue easily to summit (3–4h. to Kl. see; 3–4h. from start of climb).

West Pillar. *A good route, steep and exposed. A fair selection of pegs and a few wedges should be taken. About 300m., V, A2, with a short section of VI. First ascent: N. Baumann and Moses Gamma, 25 August, 1960.*

274. Follow Route 273 to the Kl. See and from there to the foot of the wall. This wall is marked by two distinct pillars. Start the climb in a gully which rises between a zone of slabs and the R-hand pillar. Ascend this gully easily for one rope length, then climb on the L-hand side for about 20m. Now traverse L for 10m. to reach a small rock outcrop, then climb for 15m. to a small stance. Climb the overhang above, and reach a good stance after a few m. Now climb out to the R and reach a good stance on the very edge of the pillar. Continue directly upwards for a further rope length, then go up a thin crack to a small stance. Follow this crack to its top, then traverse round L for 20m. to a small stance (VI−). Climb for 20m. (stance), then for a further 20m. and up a chimney to a large grassy zone. Traverse 20m. R and finally climb the summit wall to top (6–7h.).

Descent.

275. Either descend the upper section of Route 273 by abseiling, then down through the couloir to the Kl. See; or follow the NE ridge easily down to Höreli. From Höreli bear N for a short distance then descend over rocks E to meet the path which runs down above the Entschigtal to Wassen. From several places on the E ridge it is possible to climb or abseil down to reach the original ascent route via Rorstäfel (Route 273).

MEIGGELENSTOCK 2448.5/2416m.

A fairly long rock ridge, NE of the Salbit hut, running from the Bandlückli ENE for about 800m. Till recently very infrequently visited.

South Wall. *This would appear to be an excellent route, but the author has failed to find anyone who has repeated it and could not himself find it in 1962. Pegs and plenty of wedges should be taken. Approx. 250m., V, A1. First ascent: Sepp Inwyler and F. Haider, 1957.*

276. From the Salbit hut follow the track which runs at first E, then up N over steep grass to the foot of the rocks (45 min). The route starts in a line with a distinct 30m. dièdre rising in a series of slabs in the middle of the wall. At the foot of the wall two narrow cracks lead to a horizontal crack. Climb the L-hand crack (pegs and wedges) to a good stance at the foot of the 30m. dièdre. Follow this for a third of its height (pegs), then take a narrow crack on the L-hand wall (good holds). Climb the next short slab to a horizontal crack which is followed R to a stance. Go up R over a projecting bulge (pegs) for a few m. to reach a stance on a ledge. Traverse this ledge R to a cracked slab and climb this, bearing R at first, then L to a stance below a short overhanging crack. This is climbed to the top (wedges). Above are two parallel cracks; take the R-hand one (wedges). Finally climb a series of slabs to top (3–4h. from foot of wall).

South-East Wall (to pt.2448.5m.). *A very good route on perfect rock, Pegs and wedges necessary. 250m., about 7 rope lengths. V/V— First ascent: Moses Gamma and Geny Steiger, 14 June, 1967.*

277. From the Salbit hut follow Route 276 to the foot of the wall. Start to the R of a yellowish-brown pillar and climb a dièdre for 25m.; good stance just to L. Now climb a delicate slab for 6m., then slant R easily to a slabby groove which leads up L to a second stance. Climb the dièdre above for 8m. then slant L over slabs to the third stance below a steep barrier. Traverse

R for 12m. over a delicate slab, then climb a steep crack to the fourth stance. From here climb 3m. R, then up steep slabs in a groove for 20m. Now go R to the fifth stance, a large pulpit. Finally climb for at least 2 rope lengths up a series of cracks and slabs on excellent rock to summit (3–4h.).

West Ridge. *An interesting easy scramble; also the descent route to the Salbit hut. 400m. long, I/II.*

278. From the Salbit hut go N past the lake at pt.2047m. and climb easily to the Bandlückli, 2357m. This saddle is easily recognised as being the deepest gap in the ridge at this pt. Now follow the crest of the ridge to highest pt. of the Meiggelenstock, turning the first large rock tower on N (L) side (1–2h.).

NOTE
The famous Salbitschijen mtn. adjoining the group described in this section of the guidebook is included in the sub-area guide entitled *Engelhörner and Salbitschijen*.

PART VI

GLETSCHHORN–WINTERSTOCK GROUP

A small compact group lying immediately E of the Tiefen-stock and just N of the Furka pass above Realp. The Albert Heim hut situated at the foot of this cirque is ideally placed and all climbs are reached easily. For those who prefer to camp there are several perfect and unobtrusive sites.

Several easy and relatively short passes intersect the area, affording convenient access to and from the Göschener Tal. If the Winterlücke and Lochberglücke are used there are none of the usual glacier complications.

Although there is a good varied selection of rock climbing, from easy ridge scrambles to grade VI, the main emphasis is on higher grade climbs. The Gletschhorn S ridge (III) is a classic; the Graue Wand (VI) is one of the more recent extreme routes. The rock is granite and of the best quality.

OBER GLETSCHJOCH   c.3155m.

The deepest gap in ridge between the Tiefenstock and the Gletschhorn; lying immediately E of the Dammazwillinge W summit, pt.3275m. Not marked on LK.1:50,000, but named on LK.1:25,000. It affords an interesting glacier traverse from the Albert Heim hut to the Damma hut or vice versa; though not so direct as the Winterlücke. (Route 299). Easy on the Albert Heim side (S) and only moderate on the Damma side (N). First crossing S to N: Sir Martin Conway and E. A. Fitzgerald with two guides and two Gurkhas, 21 July, 1894. This party traversed the Nägelisgrätli from the Grimsel; crossed the Rhone glacier; climbed the Galenstock; descended to the Tiefen glacier; ascended the Damma glacier and finally walked through the Göschener Tal to Göschenen. An incredible display of stamina! *Diagram, p.148.*

279. From Albert Heim hut. From the hut follow Route 282 to the Tiefen glacier. Continue over easy névé below the walls of the Gletschhorn to a pt. below the joch; easily recognised as

145

a deep gap. Climb the snow couloir (not very steep) which runs directly up to the saddle; or climb broken rocks on E (R) side. This latter course is not really recommended (1½–2h from hut.)

280. From Damma hut. From the hut descend S to pt.2232m Cross a tributary of the Dammareuss (torrent) then climb to the rognon pt.2372.8m.; the Gemschistöckli. Now rise across the Damma glacier SW towards pt.2916m; the lowest part of the NE ridge of the Dammazwillinge W summit, 3275m., which projects far into the glacier.

To the L of this ridge is a fairly steep snow couloir rising to gap in the ridge. Cross a bergschrund and climb the couloir direct, or when it is icy, as it often is, use rocks either to L or R (2–3h. from hut).

GLETSCHHORN   3305m.

A rock peak situated NW of the Albert Heim hut. An important mtn. with a variety of interesting climbs. The rock is excellent granite and the climbs are quite near the hut.

South-West Wall. *One of the easiest routes on the mtn. short and interesting and often used for descent.* I/II. *First descended by E. Huber with J. Gamma, 12 September, 1889 Diagram, p.148.*

281. From the Albert Heim hut follow Route 282 to below gap in S ridge. Trend somewhat L over a short snowfield to foot of SW wall. At the uppermost W edge of the snowfield climb a smooth slabby groove (in descent, abseil) leading into the wall. Now continue on perfect rock (good holds) in a more or less direct line to summit (2½–3h. from hut).

South Ridge. *A fine climb, classic.* III. *First ascent: Helene Kuntze with Joseph and Gabriel Lochmatter, 22 July, 1903 Diagram, p.148.*

282. From the Albert Heim hut cross scree W to the rock

utcrop pt.2713.2m. which lies to the N (R) side of the Tiefen
lacier and below the snowy cwm formed by pt.2929m. (L)
nd the SE rib (R). Go up to the rocks of pt.2929m., then bear
on to the Tiefen glacier. Slant up keeping close to the rocks
R), then work up in a N direction, passing below a distinct
ock tower (R) till level with a gap in ridge above (R). Climb
asily to this gap, then follow the ridge which soon steepens;
xcellent rock. Continue upwards in the same line to reach
steep "impasse", which is turned on L by a steep difficult
ièdre; crux. Above this there are no further difficulties to top
–4h. from hut).

North-West Ridge. *A pleasant straightforward climb, recom-
ended if a descent is made by the E ridge (Route 284) to the
nter Gletschjoch. If the traverse of the Winterstock's three
ummits (Routes 292/3/5) is also included it affords a splendid
ng mountaineering expedition with no undue difficulties.
II. First ascent: V. de Beauclair and R. Helbling, 12 June, 1901.
iagram, p.148.*

83. From the Ober Gletschjoch (Route 279) follow the ridge
asily to the first buttress-like barrier which nearly forms a
ubsidiary summit. Climb the lower section direct then about
0m. below the highest pt. traverse N (L) along a terrace, then
egain the ridge immediately above the steep section by an
bvious chimney. Now follow the ridge directly and without
omplications to top (4½–5h. from Albert Heim hut).

East Ridge. *An easy but interesting climb. Especially recom-
ended in conjunction with the NW ridge (Route 283) and a
raverse of the Winterstock (Route 292/3/5). I/II. First descended
y V. de Beauclair and R. Helbling, 12 June, 1901 (after ascent
f NW ridge). Diagram, p. 148.*

84. From the Albert Heim hut following Route 290 to the
Unter Gletschjoch. Now climb the ridge, turning the first
eries of towers on the N (R) side. Continue up the broken
idge, now avoiding small towers and pinnacles when

Gletschhorn · Winterstock S

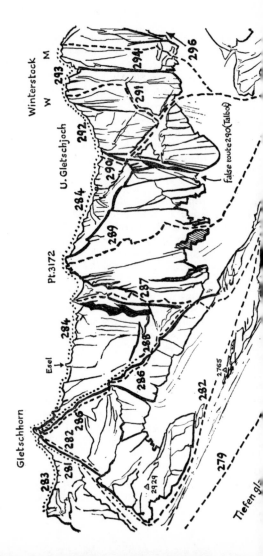

cessary on the S (L) side. At three-quarter distance pass a
nspicuous tower, easily seen from below, the 'Esel'; some
ubt exists whether this has been climbed or not. After the
sel' climb the final up-thrust to summit somewhat on the
side, then exit through a gully to top (5h. from hut).

orth Face by North Rib. *A more difficult route than the
iginal line made by E. Huber and J. Gamma, but a first-class
imb and safer from stonefall.* III/IV. *First ascent: E. Gassler
d W. Kohler, 8 July, 1934.*

5. From the Damma hut follow Route 280 as far as the Ober
letschjoch. Do not go up to pt.2916m. but before this bear
(SE) to foot of a rock rib rising towards the E ridge. The two
ms formed by this rib and that of pt.2916m. form a definite
owy cwm. Climb steep difficult rocks directly up a steep,
arrow snow/ice crest to below a huge vertical slab. Climb a
arrow chimney, then excellent rock for a short way to a second
aarp snow/ice rib. After this continue up steep rock always
eeping somewhat on the L, to join the E ridge just L of some
ellow rock towers. Follow this to summit or descend to the
nter Gletschjoch (Route 284) (6–8h. from hut).

outh-East Rib. *A very good route on excellent rock.* IV; *though
e direct finish is more difficult,* V. *First ascent: Carl E. Weber
d Max Hotz, 19 August, 1944. Diagram, p.148.*

36. From the Albert Heim hut follow Route 282 to pt. 2713.2m.
ow bear R to reach the foot of the rock spur which forms the
xtreme L edge of the snowy cwm below the SE wall. Go a
w m. L (W) round the corner of the buttress then climb a
teep 30m. dièdre to a large grassy terrace. Traverse this L
r about 10m., then climb steep perfect rock on good holds to
ach the top of the buttress. Now go up easy scree or snow to
e foot of a large distinct tower, which is separated from the
ue SE rib by an obvious gap. Climb the tower on its L edge,
en descend steeply to gap below. Follow the jagged edge,
voiding the crest, to reach the true SE rib, which is then

climbed on steep excellent rock to a large slab, not far belo
the pt. where the rib merges into the S ridge. Either travers
off without difficulty to the S ridge, which is easy; or climb
slab on the L side by a crack, then up a long dièdre with tw
overhangs running down from the S ridge. Climb this dièdr
(pegs, combined tactics) to below a large roof, then make a
exposed traverse R up to the summit ridge (4–5h. from hut

East Ridge Pillar. *A splendid climb on perfect rock. 400m
V+. First ascent: Max Niedermann and Ralf Deseke, Ju
1962. First British ascent: J. O. Talbot with Martin Epp, 196
Diagram, p.148.*

287. The pillar can easily be seen from the Albert Heim hu
lying to the L of the Graue Wand (Route 289) and culminatin
at a sharp pt. just L of pt.3172m.; the highest central pt. in th
Gletschhorn–Winterstock traversing ridge. From the hut go u
scree or snow past pt.2693m. to the R of the entrance of th
cwm formed by the Gletschhorn (L) and pt.3172m. (R). Th
foot of the pillar lies immediately to your R.

Climb on to rocks which project furthest into the sma
glacier, then traverse R for about 10m. across smooth compac
rock to a small but unmistakable dièdre; climb this for abou
12m. Before the rock becomes too difficult and overhangin
traverse L for about 3m. to a crack and climb this (pegs) to
good stance on a grassy ledge. Now climb for a rope lengt
to a series of unclimbable slabs, then go R to reach a goo
stance at the foot of a dièdre. Climb this for about 20m. (pegs
to below a roof.

Climb the roof (pegs), then 20m. free up a steep difficult wa
to a stance. Climb direct for one rope length, bearing R belov
a rocky buttress to a ledge; stance. Go 5m. L to a large cracke
slab and climb this by the crack between the wall and the slab
Continue up for about 20–25m. and climb the next wall to reac
a groove that runs up through the shoulder of the pillar. Clim
fairly easily for at least three rope lengths till the rock become
very steep and difficult. Go R but as soon as possible befor

the wall falls away too steeply go up a short pitch to a stance. Climb a crack for 10m,; make a difficult, delicate traverse R, then descend a little in a groove into a gap in the ridge. From here climb on the W (L) side for one rope length, then once more return R and after two rope lengths reach the E ridge which is followed to summit (7–8h. from hut).

South-East Wall. *This wall, between the SE rib and E ridge, is divided into three sections. A lower 60m. topped by a large scree terrace which cuts right across the face; a middle 200m. wall section; a second but smaller recession and the final steep upper wall of approx. 100–120m. The rock is excellent and the climbing good and interesting, but it is a pity that the face is so broken. The route description is vague in places and the start is not easy to find. IV/V+. First ascent: Max Niedermann, Axel Pauls and Werner Sieber, 13 June, 1964. Diagram, p.148.*

288. Reach the foot of the wall in about 45min. from the Albert Heim hut (NW) over the small glacier R of the SE rib (Route 286). Cross a schrund then slant R for approx. 60m. towards the gully coming down from the E ridge (R). A yellow 3–10m. slab marks the start, varying according to snow conditions. Climb this, traverse a few m. L, then take a slab R to below a steep section cut by a tiny shallow crack. Take this crack (pegs), traverse 8m. L then climb another steep wall by a second crack to the great terrace.

Climb over scree/snow towards a large block, and from this climb old snow for 30m. From the top of the snow climb a 4–10m. dièdre (depending on conditions) to a small terrace with a niche and small cairn. Go L round the corner of the niche then climb 25–30m. (pegs) to a stance on another small terrace. Now climb a 15m. wall (pegs), then move R to a detached slab; stance. Continue up, bearing R, for several rope-lengths till the upper wall can be seen, then climb directly to below it in several rope lengths.

Climb a short steep wall at its foot (2 pegs), then go up a double dièdre (6 pegs) which narrows after 8–10m. to a wide crack, to reach a stance on a small terrace (2 wedges). Continue direct for a rope length to a stance on a distinct rock rib on the wall; finally climb this for 50m. to top (4–5h. from foot of face).

'Graue Wand' or South Wall. *A splendid climb on perfect rock; steep, difficult and sustained. 400m., VI. First ascent: Max Niedermann, Werner Sieber and Heinz Stähli, 13/14 September, 1964. The 'Graue Wand' forms the S wall of pt.3172m. on the E ridge. It lies R of the E ridge pillar (Route 287) and is easily recognised. At the base of the wall are two distinct rock buttresses, projecting into the snow; to get on to the face it is necessary to climb the lower R-hand pillar to reach a prominent crack which rises from L to R. Diagram, p.148.*

289. From the Albert Heim hut follow Route 287 as for the E ridge pillar. Bear off R before reaching this pillar, then cross snow and scree to arrive at the foot of the Graue Wand R-hand pillar (30–40min.). Traverse L across slabs and reach a short crack which leads to the start of a gully. Continue up this over a series of rocky steps to the true start of the wall and a belaying peg.

From the peg go directly up a crack which leads up slabs for 35m. to a stance. Go up a few m. L, then return to the crack and continue up for half a rope length to a second stance, below an overhang. Climb this, go up a thin, shallow, parallel crack in slabs for about 20m., then traverse L back to the original crack; stance. Now climb a difficult slightly overhanging crack for 30–35m. to an étrier stance; 2 good pegs. Ascend L in a dièdre, then return to the crack which is followed to a stance about 3m. below an overhang. Take this L by a crack then go up slabs for a rope length to a ledge; stance. Now move L over slabby rock by a short crack to a stance. Cross a slab for about 4m. on good holds to a small crystal hole; climb up this for 5m.; traverse R for 2m., then climb for 8m. in a somewhat grassy crack to a ledge; stance. Bivouac place of first ascensionists.

From the L end of the ledge climb a crack, then a ribbed

ridge for a rope length to a stance. Make a difficult step into a crack and climb this to a second similar ridge. From its upper section traverse up L in a wide crack, then go up rocky steps for 35m. to below a dièdre; stance. Climb the dièdre to its top and reach a ledge. Traverse L for 4–5m., then go up to a stance on another ledge. Traverse L for 3m., then climb the next steep slabby wall for 35m. to a series of blocks; stance. Climb a crack for 30m., go L and ascend parallel to a crack; stance. Continue to a gap; pass this 3m. below to the R, over a slab; then directly up to summit (20h. for first ascent. 50–55 pegs and 5 wedges).

UNTER GLETSCHJOCH   c.3080m.

The deepest gap in the Gletschhorn E ridge, between pt.3172m. and the Winterstock; approx. 400m. W of the W summit. Not marked on LK.1:50,000 but named on the recent LK.1:25,000. Its main use is for access to and from the Gletschhorn and Winterstock. It is rarely used as a pass from the Albert Heim hut to the Göschener Tal, as the latter side is long, complicated and dangerous from stonefall. The key part of the route is a distinct rocky rib running NNW from the Winterstock. First ascended by F. F. Tuckett with Christian and Peter Michel. *Diagram, p.148.*

290. From the Albert Heim hut go into the glacier cwm SW of the Winterstock. Cross to the upper L-hand corner of the snow-field, then climb easy slabs to reach a large distinct terrace; snow or scree. Traverse up L to a gully which leads up slanting somewhat R to the joch above. The foot of this gully lies in a more or less direct line with pt.2713.2m.; the rognon in the Tiefen glacier (2½–3h. from hut).
N.B. Do not descend or ascend the continuation of the couloir which runs directly down to the Tiefen glacier; difficult and dangerous; descended in error by author in 1962.

WINTERSTOCK   3203m.

A fine triple-headed rock peak situated NW and within easy access of the Albert Heim hut. There is a good selection of ridge and wall climbs, from I–VI, forming an ideal climbing ground for everyone. Routes from the Göschener side have been omitted because access and approach are both long and difficult and the climbs inferior to those from the Albert Heim. The summit needle of the W summit, first climbed by Alfred Amstad and Guido Masetto, 21 August, 1935, is taken on the N side and finally on its E edge. Very difficult and delicate.

South Wall (West Summit). *No height on LK. A good, interesting and recommended climb.* III. *First ascent: Alfred Amstad and Guido Masetto, 21 August, 1935. Diagram, p.148.*

291. From the Albert Heim hut follow Route 290 to the upper corner of the snowfield, to a pt. below the S wall. Climb steep slabs to a terrace which is turned E (R) to reach a niche. Go L from the niche, then up a chimney dièdre to a stance. Climb direct on steep, somewhat poor rock till it is possible to reach an obvious rock rib R. Follow this steeply and pleasantly to just below the summit, then go a little E (R) and so reach top (2–3h. from foot).

West Ridge (West Summit). *A fairly easy but entertaining climb.* I/II. *First descended by V. de Beauclair and Th. Herzog, 30 July, 1902. Diagram, p.148.*

292. From the Albert Heim hut follow Route 290 to the Unter Gletschjoch, then climb the ridge to three rock towers. The first two are turned on the N (L) side, the third on the S (R). Now continue up the ridge to the final steep, slabby 'impasse'. Either climb it direct by a chimney or avoid on the S side. Above this climb the ridge for a short distance and finally up a slab to top (1–1½h. from joch).

Traverse from W to main Summit (3203m.) *Normally quite easy; can be tricky when icy or after fresh snowfall.* I/II. *Diagram, p.148.*

293. From the W summit descend a vague couloir on the S side to reach a terrace which runs to the gap between the two summits. Now follow a sloping terrace. somewhat icy, on to the N side of the main peak, then climb a short chimney. Go up a small ledge and a series of large blocks to reach summit (1–2h.).

South Wall (Main Summit). *An easy climb taking a fine direct line; interesting, I/II. As snow is apt to remain on ledges it is best done when completely free otherwise it can be very slippery. First ascent: Alfred and Otto Amstad and Frank Strauss, 9 August, 1936. Diagram, p.148.*

294. From the Albert Heim hut follow Route 290 into the glacier cwm SW of the Winterstock. Slant up R to foot of the wall at the head of the snowfield. Climb easy rocks bearing somewhat R to reach the fairly steep but easy concave wall. Go up in a more or less direct line to summit above; the rocks are easy but often snow-flecked (2–2½h. from foot).

North-East Ridge (Main Summit) *A good climb and quite difficult. II/III. First ascent: Val Fynn and P. Goudet, 28 February, 1891.*

295. From the Albert Heim hut follow Route 299 to the Winterlücke. Now climb the ridge crest over blocks and slabs on good rock to the final steep step before the summit. Traverse L, then regain the ridge and climb it to the top. It is also possible to avoid the difficulties of the crest by following the ridge below on the S side, but this defeats the object (2–2½h. from lücke).

South-West Couloir. *A quick descent or ascent route especially in good snow conditions. I. First descended by Ed. Wagner, L. Zündel and R. Helbling, 16 July, 1899. Diagram, p.148.*

296. Follow Route 294 as for the S wall, then slant R to foot of a snow couloir which rises to gap between the two summits; the main and S. Climb the couloir to top, then if there is sufficient snow climb directly over it to summit. If not there is a steep smooth slab which is avoided by descending E for about 50m. then climbing back up easy rock to top. In descent it is best to abseil down this slab (1½–2h. from foot, or quicker depending on conditions).

South Ridge (South Summit). *Pt.3176.3m. An easy climb; very useful for a descent after the SE ridge (Route 298).* I/II. *First ascent: V. de Beauclair and Th. Herzog, 30 July, 1902.*

297. From the Albert Heim hut follow Route 299 for the Winterlücke to below the 'Sunnig Berg', pt.2731m. Ascend this easily L then go up a wide couloir, faint track in places, to join the ridge. Avoid the first large step on W (R) or E (L), then follow the rocky ridge without difficulty to top (3h. from hut).

South-East Ridge (South Summit). *This is without doubt the finest and most difficult route in the Winterstock group. The ridge is 1000–1100m. long with an approx. vertical interval of 600m. The two towers afford 500m. of splendid sustained climbing.* VI. *First ascent: Max Niedermann and Werner Sieber. Axel Pauls was a partner on the first tower; August, 1965.*

298. From the Albert Heim hut follow Route 299 as for the Winterlücke. After passing the 'Sunnig Berg', pt.2731m., go N towards the lücke for a short distance then bear up L towards the foot of the first tower of the SE ridge. This is not difficult and the towers are easily recognised (1–1½h.).

Avoid a large obvious chimney, loose and wet; start the climb 8–10m. to its R. Climb a crack direct for 20–25m. (pegs), then a steep, difficult wall above to a stance, awkward strata. Go L and up a dièdre to its top (pegs), then traverse L to a ledge and stance. Climb difficult rock direct for 35m. (pegs) to a stance. From here go L and up a gully for 25m., then traverse on to the L wall and so reach a small crystal hole; stance. Now climb a 15m. dièdre to a stance on the tower edge. A further 5m. then move L to a stance (pegs). Climb the next corner crack direct for about 10m., then go on to the L wall to a steep ramp which is climbed to its top; stance. Cross easily downwards (L) for a few m., then climb direct for 30m.

with a stance L on a ledge. Climb the slab L for 15m. direct,
then L round a corner and up an 8m. wall (pegs); stance up to
R. Now go up L and climb a dièdre which leads to gap behind
the first tower. Go through the gap and emerge on the N (R)
side of the ridge. Avoid the first rocky teeth on the ridge (R);
from the next gap reach the crest after 10m. Follow the crest
without much difficulty for 3–4 rope lengths to the large main
saddle before the second tower. It is possible to get off the
ridge here by either descending a snow couoir N (R) towards
the Winterlücke or S (L) by a similar couloir.

From the saddle climb direct for 40m. to a large boulder-
strewn terrace (peg); then go up a 5m. wall to a ledge which
cuts across the face. Climb a narrow crack which widens after
3m. (pegs and wedges) for about 30m. to a peg. Continue direct
for 6–7m., then cross L to a crack which leads up L to a dièdre
(pegs, wedges); étrier stance. Climb this dièdre 6–7m.
(wedges), then move 2m. on to the R wall and go up a crack.
At its top make an awkward move L to get back into the dièdre.
Continue up the wide chimney-like crack at the back of the
dièdre to a poor stance. Continue upwards for a further
3–4m., then traverse L over the overhanging dièdre wall and
climb a crack to the height of the dièdre (pegs and wedges).
Now climb the R wall (4 bolts), up a compact slab and then L
to below an overhang; étrier stance. Traverse R below this
overhang (wedges) and at its R end go up a dièdre (wedges);
good stance after 30m. on a ledge. Climb a short 8m. wall and
reach the upper ridge of the second tower. A further 35–40m.
leads to its top.

Now abseil 35m. on the R side of the ridge, thus avoiding the
first rocky towers; the second section can be climbed. Continue down for a further 15m. to the deepest gap in the ridge
after the second tower, then keeping sometimes on the R
side, sometimes on the crest, follow the ridge to S summit
(18h. for first ascent).

WINTERLÜCKE 2854m.

An easy pass between the Winterstock and the Lochberg. A

popular and convenient way between the Albert Heim hut and the Göschener Tal. It is frequently used from Realp at the foot of the Furka pass; the path joining the same route as that from the Albert Heim hut.

299. From Albert Heim hut. From the hut descend (E) in the narrow deep-cut valley which runs immediately N of the hut. After passing round the rocky spur of the Sunnig Berg, pt.2731m., go N through a narrow valley with roches moutonnées to below an easy snow slope. Ascend this direct to pass (2h. from hut).

300. From Göschener Tal. Follow the hut path for the Damma hut to the E side of the Dammareuss (torrent). Now ascend easily SW over moraine to below pt.2374m. (LK.1:25,000), then go up directly over easy rock or snow to the lücke. If there is any avalanche danger or conditions are icy it is best to follow the distinct rocky rib of the Winteregg which runs just W of the normal route (3–4h. from Göscheneralpsee–Dam).

LOCHBERG   3074.2m.

The most easterly mtn. in the Gletschhorn–Winterstock group yet within easy access of the Albert Heim hut. The routes from the Winterlücke and Lochberglücke are easy scrambles and are best used for descent after the SW wall; the only really good climb on the mtn. The approach from the Göschener Tal is tedious, long and monotonous and is seldom used. First ascent: Carl Seelig and Aug Naef, 24 July, 1887.

South-West Wall. *A good climb, not sustained but with some excellent pitches. 250m. IV/V. First ascent: S. Inwyler and F. Haider, 1958. Climbed by J. O. Talbot and Martin Epp, 3 September, 1968.*

301. From the Albert Heim hut follow Route 299 into the small valley before the Winterlücke. Now bear up steeply R (NNE) to pt. 2548m.; faint track in places. From here go NNW to snow slopes below the Lochberg, the bottom of which is divided into three triangular-shaped rock walls.

Cross hard fairly steep snow to the L edge of the middle rock wall and climb a short buttress-like ramp to reach the start of the climb. Climb a slab R, then continue making a rising traverse R by a thin corner crack below a slightly overhanging wall for a rope-length to a stance; one peg, awkward and difficult. Now climb an obvious black dièdre direct to a stance. Above this slant L over easy ground to foot of a steep grey wall cut by an open dièdre. Climb a short overhanging slab then go up the dièdre steeply but on excellent rock for one rope-length to a tiny stance. Make an awkward move R then climb direct to a deep-cut dièdre with an overhang.

Climb the overhang free by bridging, then up the steep but progressively easier crack to a good stance at the top of the grey wall. Go round the corner L, climb a short crack, then up the crest of the spiky ridge above to a gap before the final upthrust to summit.

Descend a short distance R then ascend the wall, slanting up R to a good stance below two obvious dièdres. Climb the R-hand dièdre, difficult at the top, to flat blocks of the summit ridge. Now follow snow R of the rocks to main summit (5–6h. from hut).

From the Winterlücke. *An easy route, but one extremely difficult to follow in bad weather. The constant tendency is to bear too far L or R, either ending up in the wrong valley or among precipitous cliffs.* l.

302. From the Winterlücke follow the W ridge to the first steep step. Avoid this (S) by a wide scree snow couloir which leads up to below the summit block. The step can also be turned to the N (30–40 min. from lücke).

From the Lochberglücke. *Another easy route, but as the ridge is longer and the lücke itself is further from the Albert Heim it is not so popular as Route 302.* l.

303. From the Lochberglücke (Route 304) follow the SE ridge pleasantly over rock and snow, finally over an easy snowfield to summit block (1½h. from lücke).

PLANGGENSTOCK   2823.3m.

HÖHENBERG   2361m.

Two minor unimportant mtns. without mountaineering interest, lying N of the Lochberglücke.

LOCHBERGLÜCKE   c.2815m.

Not marked on LK.1:50,000 but named on LK.1:25,000. An easy direct pass connecting the Albert Heim and the Göschener Tal; it lies between the Lochberg and the Blauberg. The route on the N side is difficult to find in bad weather.

304. From Albert Heim hut. From the hut follow Route 301 to pt.2548m. Now continue slanting NE over a series of ledges, easy rocks and snow to the lücke (2½h. from hut).

305. From Göschener Tal. From the dam of the Göschener-alpsee follow path to the Damma hut for a short distance till it levels by a small wooden bridge. Cross the bridge and ascend the valley S on the W side of the stream, over the 'Älpergen platten' (slab) to the 'Älpergensee' (lake), pt.2515m. (LK.1:50,000), 2510m. (LK.1:25,000). Continue up past pt.2576m. (LK.1:25,000), then bear up SW over easy slabs and snow to pass (3½h. from the dam).

PART VII

FELDSCHIJEN–MÜETERLISHORN GROUP

A complex, hitherto little-known and unfrequented area running due E from the Gletschhorn–Winterstock group. There are no huts and access from the Göschener Tal (N) and Urseren (S) is somewhat long and strenuous, making it very much the preserve of weekend climbers and not foreign visitors.

Both the quality of the climbs and the rock is good and there is little doubt that they will become progressively more popular, like such areas as the Bergseeschijen and Büelenhorn. It is essential that the new large scale LK.1:25,000 map is used because the ridges, facets and passes are so clearly shown. All references are to this map and not the old LK.1:50,000.

Apart from technical climbing skill, mountaineering experience is often required to find the climbs and to follow routes which have been infrequently repeated. There are no glacier complications, but a short ice axe could be useful for descending steep gullies and couloirs where there may be an accumulation of old snow. As access is fairly difficult, high-level camping is really the ideal answer for those who wish to climb in these wild and unspoilt rock mtns. Camping provisions can be bought at Realp, Hospental, Andermatt, or Göschenen but not in the Göschener Tal. The restaurant at the Göschener-alpsee can only supply chocolate, biscuits and similar items.

AELPERGENLUCKE   2782m.

A pass between the Blauberg and pt.2865.2m., affording an easy and popular route between the Göschener Tal and Realp.

Ascent from Göschener Tal and descent to Realp.

306. From the dam of the Göscheneralpsee follow Route 305 to pt. 2576m., then bear up slightly SSE and finally cross easy snow to the pass (3h.). From the lücke descend scree, rock, or snow easily SE past the 2500m. contour to pt.2350m. Now descend SW past Obergadmen to join the Albert Heim hut path which is followed down to Realp (1½–2h.).

BLAUBERG   2955m.

This mtn. consists of a long horizontal ridge with a distinct E summit needle. The route of the first ascensionists by the E ridge from the Blauberglücke is of no interest and is seldom done; the only climb of merit is the SW wall with a descent to the Alpergenlücke (Aelpergenlücke). First ascent: Paul Schucan and Hans Hössli, June, 1903.

South-West Wall (to E Needle). *A good interesting climb, the best on the mtn.* III. *First ascent: Nik. Meyer and Hans Iten, 1944.*

307. From Realp ascend the descent of Route 306 as far as the 2500m. contour, then bear up R over the small glacier at the foot of the SW wall. The climb starts where the snow reaches highest up into the wall. Climb a chimney and reach a scree terrace, then go up direct till it is possible to move R and reach a slabby gully, Follow a dièdre, then traverse a narrow ledge L and over an awkward slab with a prominent bulge to easier rock. Arrive at another slab and avoid this L by descending about 6m. to reach a niche beside a chimney. Climb this to a terrace, then climb a short 3m. wall direct. Now take a difficult exposed chimney which leads up R, followed by 20m. up L, then up a slab on good holds to a ridge edge. A crack leads to a platfrom stance above. Climb a difficult narrow 12m. chimney, then go along a narrow ledge NW to reach a crack which leads to a gap NW of the summit needle. From here go R on to the wall and finally climb a crack to top of the needle; room only for two people (6–8 h. from Realp).

Descent by SW ridge to Aelpergenlücke. Keep to the S (L) side of the ridge as far as a deep gap. From here follow the narrow crest of a blocky ridge to the lücke (1½h.).

BLAUBERGLÜCKE   c.2925m.

308. Not marked on LK. The deepest gap in the ridge between the Blauberg (2955m.) and the Müeterlishorn W summit (3039m.). It is sometimes but rarely used as a pass between

Realp and the Göschener Tal; its main function is a means of access to and from the Müeterlishorn.

From pt.2350m. (S side, Route 306) go more or less directly N over a small glacier nearly to its head, then climb up L (WNW) over easy rocks to the lücke (3–4h. from Realp).

From pt.2510m. on the N side climb SE over snow and scree, then finally a short section of rocks to reach the lücke without difficulty (2–2½h. from the dam).

MÜETERLISHORN 3066m.

A long, complex mtn. NE, of the Blauberg. There are three main summits; the West, the Main and the East, each with a bewildering array of minor peaks and secondary ridges. The W summit (3039m.) lies NE of the Blauberglücke; the Main (3066m.) ENE of the W; and the E, (3058.7m.) ENE from the Main and S from the Müeterlissattel, There is a wide variety of climbs and each summit has been treated as a separate entity with the most important routes. Several combinations of traverses are possible.

West Summit 3039m.

South-West Ridge. *A good short interesting climb.* II/III. *First ascent: Julius Heller and W. Fuchs, September 1913. Diagram, p.169.*

309. From the Blauberglücke (Route 308) climb the ridge to below a large overhanging block. Traverse SE then go up a steep exposed chimney to a shoulder. Move E for 8–10m. along a good ledge then rejoin the ridge without difficulty and follow it over a series of large blocks to top (1½–2h. from Blauberglücke).

North-West Ridge. *The best and most difficult climb on this summit. The ridge is dominated by a prominent subsidiary summit, approx. 2997m., and the difficulties of the route are in climbing it. Above this pt. there are no complications.* IV—. *First ascent: Louis Meyer, Jean Fritsch and Emil J. Meyer, 15 August, 1913. Diagram, p.169.*

310. From the Göscheneralpsee dam follow Route 305 to pt.2510m. and the little lake of the Älpergensee. Now ascend SE and go up an easy blocky ridge to the start of the climb, in direct line with the obvious secondary summit. Climb the first step direct for a few m., then slant slightly W (R), then return to the direct line. Now climb to a large projecting slab, easily seen from below. This is the key to the lower part of the climb. Ascend the edge of this slab *à cheval*, then mount easier rocks to the first cracked tower of the ridge.

Climb the crack which splits it for about half-height, then go round on the N side and thus avoid the next tower. Before the third tower descend for 15m. on to the S wall, then traverse horizontally to reach a crack which is climbed to its top. Go through a form of rocky arch, then L to a hollow below the summit block. Climb a sharp exposed ridge to a good ledge and finally up another edge to top of the secondary summit. This final edge can also be climbed on the L side on good holds.

Descend to the gap immediately below this pt. by abseil and climbing, then follow the ridge without difficulty to W summit (6–7h. from the dam).

Main Summit.   3066m.

From W summit by West Ridge. *A pleasant, interesting traverse.* II/III. *First ascent: V. de Beauclair, Fr. Weber and R. v Wyss, 6 July, 1902. Diagram, p.169.*

311. From the W summit descend the E ridge to within a short distance of the gap between the two summits, then go R(S) and climb down keeping below the crest. It is also possible from the Blauberglücke to traverse across the S wall to reach the gap. From here descend on to the S wall, climbing a steep 4m. step by a crack, to reach a horizontal ledge. From here get on to the W ridge and climb it to the main summit (2½h. from summit to summit).

North-East Wall. *A simple climb; short and useful for descent:* II. *First descended by Paul and Charles Montandon, 29 June, 1902. Diagram, p.169.*

312. From the Göscheneralpsee follow Route 305 to pt.2510m. Go SE to the diminutive Blauberg glacier (usually old snow and scree) and climb this to the old glacier cwm between the Main and E summits. Bear L to the foot of the wall and climb a wide snow or rocky couloir rising to the E ridge. Follow this to summit (4h. from dam).

North-West Wall. *Comparable to Route 312 and also useful for descent.* II. *First descended by Julius Heller and Jean Munck, 21 September, 1908. Diagram, p.169.*

313. Follow Route 312 over the Blauberg glacier, then bear R to reach the glacier cwm between the W and main summits. Cross snow to the pt. where the snow rises highest into the wall and merges into a sort of rocky couloir. Climb this, then finally quite easy rocks, always bearing R, to reach the W ridge about 40m. below summit (4–5h. from dam).

South Ridge. *A splendid climb on perfect rock; 750–800m. long with a vertical interval of 450–480m.* IV/V+. *First ascent: Max Niedermann and Sepp Renner, 12 August, 1966.*

314. From Realp go N past pt.2350m. and over the Alp Lipferstein. Continue in the same direction to the entrance of the large glacier cwm of the Main and E summits. The climb starts at the foot of a slabby wall SE of pt.2857m.; an arm of the S ridge. Climb this steep slabby wall (pegs) for 30–40m., then traverse L to a wide crack between the wall and a detached slab (1 peg). Climb the crack to a ledge and follow this L for 35m. to a stance. Now climb three rope lengths to a snow/scree hollow. Go up R towards the side of the ridge towers, then up slabs direct for 5–6m. to reach a crack which slants from R to L. Follow this to a stance (1 peg) on the ridge edge. Now traverse across on the L (W) side of the ridge to another small hollow. Exit from this up a slabby step (1 peg), then up a short dièdre (1 peg) to the ridge.

Traverse along the L side of the ridge for 2–3m. to a stance. From here climb an overhanging crack (1–2 pegs), then climb the ridge on the E (R) side to a stance. Continue for 4–5 rope lengths on the R side of the ridge to the large tower of pt.2920m. From this tower go two rope lengths along the ridge, then on the L side (W) climb down to the gap before the main summit block. Climb the ridge over a series of steep steps for two rope lengths with a final easy pitch to top (9h. for first ascent. At least 2½–3h. should be allowed from Realp to reach the start of the climb).

East Summit   3058.7m.

From Main Summit along West Ridge. *An excellent traverse when done in conjunction with Route 309 and a descent of Route 316 to the Müeterlissattel. II. First ascent of E Ridge of Main Summit: Paul and Charles Montandon, 29 July, 1902. First ascent of West Ridge of East Summit: Paul Montandon, C. Seelig and K. Knecht, 7 October, 1900. Diagram, p.169.*

315. From the Main summit follow the ridge down to the highest tower. Either abseil down it or descend R on the S side in a steep couloir to regain the ridge below; follow this down to gap between the two summits. This pt. can be easily reached from the Blauberg glacier. Now follow the W ridge easily to the E summit (1–1½h. from summit to summit).

North-West Ridge. *Quite difficult; the actual climb is short but the approach long. III. First descended by V. de Beauclair, H. Seiler and R. v Wyss, 1901. Diagram, p.169.*

316. From the Müerterlissattel (Route 320) follow the ridge direct to summit (5–6h. from Göscheneralp (N) and about same time from Realp or Hospental).

South-East Ridge. *An interesting difficult climb, but the main problem is to find the start. III. First ascent: V. de Beauclair, H. Seiler and R. v Wyss, 1901.*

317. From Zumdorf, the small village between Realp and Hospental, go up NW over the Rinbortalp to foot of the snow couloir in E side of the SE ridge, which runs close to a distinct rock tower on the ridge. Climb the couloir to the ridge and follow this to a group of large rock towers where it joins the SE ridge. Now either traverse across on the N side to below the summit and then climb direct on steep rock; or traverse for a short distance till past the towers, then return to the ridge. Continue along it to reach the gap before the summit tower, then work round N and climb a difficult tunnel-like crack to the upper ridge, thence to summit (6–7h. from Zumdorf).

East Ridge. *Similar to Route 317 but with a different approach. The first ascensionists used the easier variation. I/II. First ascent: J. Eggerman and a companion, 18 September, 1887.*

318. From the Rinbortalp (Route 317) go up to the S side of the E ridge. Climb a couloir leading to the crest then follow it to where it joins the SE ridge and the rocky towers (Route 317) (6–7h. from Zumdorf).

South Edge Direct. *A first-class route on good rock; difficult and sustained. 400m., V+, A2. First ascent: Heidi and Albin Schelbert-Syfrig, 24 October, 1965.*

319. From Realp go N past pt.2350m. and up over the Lipfersteinalp to the S ridge. The route follows the edge of two huge towers and the climb starts beside a dièdre which leads up slightly L; marker peg. Climb this dièdre to its top, then climb 30m. up L to a stance (A1, A2, V+). Go up the next white-coloured dièdre, turn a jammed block L, then up a steep 40m. crack to a stance in a funnel (V+, A2). Climb a dièdre to its top, then climb R (III, IV) to a detached block; stance. Go R and round the edge (wedges), over slabs and up L to a stance (III, IV). Climb L for 30m. along a ledge to the edge, then ascend direct in a dièdre to below an overhanging wall. Go R and up a crack to a stance (IV, A2). Climb a dièdre full of blocks to its top and slant R up a series of steps to a slab (III). Climb this on good holds to a zone of light-coloured slabs, which are climbed up L to a stance (IV, V).

Feldschijen · Müeterlishorn W

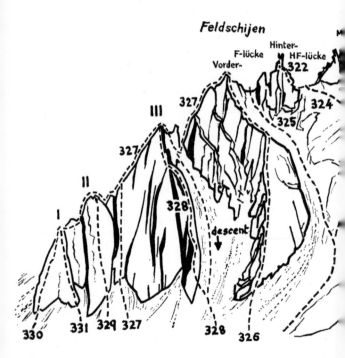

Feldschijen

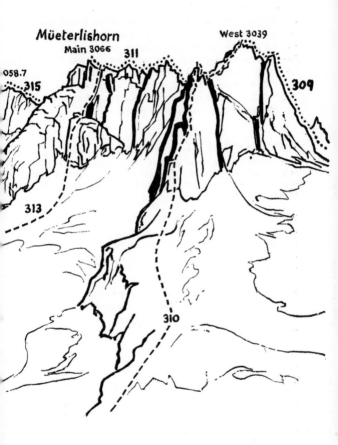

Müeterlishorn
Main 3066   311
058.7
315   West 3039   309
313
310

Descend 1m. and work E to a large dièdre which is climbed to a stance on the ridge edge (IV). Climb a 5m. slabby gendarme (V+), descend for 2m., then go up steep slabs to the horizontal ridge. Follow this on the sharp narrow crest, then avoid a large tower L and so reach a gap before another tower. Climb slabs (IV+) to a crack (rope manoeuvre) which leads up L, then finally to its top (V). Descend for a few m., then abseil R to the gap before the summit tower. Now follow Route 317 to top (8h. for first ascent from start of climb).

MÜETERLISSATTEL   c.3000m.

Not marked or named on LK. This saddle lies N of the Müeterlishorn E summit. It is rarely if ever used as a pass and only as a means of access to the Müeterlishorn, and then not often. *Diagram, p.168.*

320. From North. From the Göscheneralpsee follow Route 312 over the old bed of the Blauberg glacier, then cross the cwm of the main and E summits towards the E arm running down from the latter summit, and finally over scree and snow to saddle (3–3½h.).

321. From South. From the Rinbortalp (Route 317) work up round to NW into the cwm NE of rocks of the E Müeterlishorn. Finally go W and up a long steep couloir, usually frozen snow, to saddle (3–3½h.).

HINTER FELDSCHIJEN   3021m.

A wild impressive rock pinnacle lying due N of the Hinter Feldschijenlücke. The climbs are short but of good quality. First ascent: R. Cary Gilson, G. E. Ashford, L. G. Curtis and L. C. M. S. Amery, 25 August, 1895.

From the Hinter Feldschijenlücke. *A popular climb with two good variations.* III, *100m. Diagram, p.168.*

322. From the lücke (Route 324) climb the somewhat vague ridge up the steep blocky SW wall. Now work up to a small rock shoulder high on the W ridge. From here climb a steep 6m. crack to a horizontal slab about 15m. below the summit. There are now two ways: (i) The 'Kamin' or chimney: III+. First ascent: V. de Beauclair, Hans Biehly and R. Helbling, 23 August, 1902.

From the E end of the slab it is possible to reach an 8m. chimney. Climb this, steep and exposed, to a rock window. Now go R, then up to top (1–1½h. from start of climb).

(ii) The 'Wand' or wall: III. First ascent: O. Fischer and Fr. Weber, 30 May, 1903.

From the W end of the slab climb a short steep wall by combined tactics. Crawl under an overhanging block, then up between two large blocks to a terrace. Now a final 2m. steep step to summit (1–1½h. from start).

East Edge. *A fine classic route on excellent rock. 140m. IV/V +. First ascent : Alfred and Otto Amstad and Guido Masetto, 20 August, 1935.*

323. From the Hinter Feldschijenlücke go to the foot of the E side and ascend easy rock and scree to the start of the E *kante*. Climb for about 20m., then traverse just N of the *kante* to a difficult 40m. chimney which ends on the crest of the *kante*. Climb a block, go up L for a few m. on a cracked slab, then traverse up R on another slab to a stance. Climb cracks and cross the slabby *kante* R to reach a deep chimney. Climb this for 8m., then traverse L across a scree terrace back to the *kante* and climb a 5m. crack to a stance, 2m. above a large scree platform. Now climb R, go over a block and up to about 5m. below an obvious gap. Traverse a smooth slab R and climb a chimney to the platform before the summit wall. From here follow either of the two variations of Route 322 to top (3h. from foot of *kante*).

HINTER FELDSCHIJENLÜCKE c.2930m.

A wide saddle between the Müeterlishorn and Hinter Feldschijen, affording access to climbs on the latter peak.

Easy to reach but somewhat tiring owing to the unpleasant terrain. *Diagram, p.168.*

324. From the Göscheneralpsee follow Route 320 over the old bed of the Blauberg glacier, scree, rock and old snow, to saddle (4h. from dam).

VORDER FELDSCHIJENLÜCKE   c.2930m.

The saddle between the Vorder and Hinter Feldschijen: N of the latter peak. Easy but steep unpleasant terrain. *Diagram, p.168.*

325. Follow Route 324 but when level with the cwm of the Müeterlishorn Main and W summits (R) bear up quite steeply L to the saddle. Easily recognised by a sharp rock tower (4–4½h. from dam).

VORDER FELDSCHIJEN   2962m.

A fine impressive rock peak with three towers descending N towards the Göscheneralpsee. Nearly all the climbs are steep, difficult and exposed, but on good rock. The normal approach is from the dam wall of the Göscheneralpsee, but as this is quite long the best plan would be to camp beside the Älpergensee (Route 305).

Main Summit   2962m.

West Ridge. *A fairly popular and interesting route.* III. *First ascent: R. Helbling and H. Stamm, 30 May, 1902. Diagram, p.168.*

326. From the dam follow Route 305 towards pt.2510m. About half-way to this pt., cross the small stream and slant up L over scree and easy rocks to the ridge which is climbed to summit (4–5h. from the dam).

North Ridge with Traverse of Tower III. *An interesting, varied climb; quite long. First ascent: O. Gericht and companions, 18 July, 1943. Diagram, p.168.*

327. From the dam follow Route 305 to about the 2400m. contour, then bear L to below the couloir which runs to the gap between Towers II and III. Either climb the rock rib running up its centre or rocks on the L side to the ridge above. Climb the ridge keeping on the E side and turn the summit block of Tower III on E side. Descend E in a vague gully, then abseil for 30m. and reach a gully about 5m. below the next gap. Avoid the next tower by climbing across for 2–3m., then slant R towards the ridge edge. Continue up cracks and slabs, keeping as close to the ridge as possible, till it falls to below the summit block of pt.2935m. Traverse across on the W side to reach a small rock pinnacle. Climb this and after a few m. reach the top of pt.2935m. Now follow the W ridge without incident to main summit (5–6h. from dam).

Descent from Main summit. Follow the S ridge easily down to the Vorder Feldschijenlücke (15min.), thence by Route 325 to the Göscheneralpsee.

Tower III   2828m.

West Ridge. *A fine route on good rock. Difficut but there are several places where it is possible to get off the climb. 300m., IV/V. First ascent: A. Voit, R. Savaldelli, K. Walder and E. Benz, 1949. Diagram, p.168.*

328. Follow Route 326 as for the Main summit W ridge, then bear L to the foot of the W ridge. The climb starts somewhat on the S side beside a large block. Go a few m. L from here, then climb a rope-length to reach the sharp ridge edge. Continue up this for three rope-lengths, traverse a ledge for 20m. on to the S wall, then climb back up to rejoin the ridge. Follow it to a large buttress-like step and avoid this by traversing N (L) to reach a niche, large enough for two people (pegs). Climb straight up for 3m., steep and difficult (pegs); then slant L to a wide chimney which is climbed to the ridge; route book. Now trend up somewhat S of the ridge towards the summit block of Tower III. Climb over cracked blocks and go up a chimney on the N side to reach a ledge which runs back to the ridge. Climb this, varied and interesting, to the summit. Descend on the E side, then abseil down to gap below. Now follow the wide easy scree gully down to foot of the climb (4–5h. from start).

Tower II   2654m.

West Edge. *A splendid route; steep, difficult and sustained. 250m., V/VI. First ascent: E. Trüb and H. Horisberger, 2 June, 1963. Diagram, p. 168.*

329. Follow Route 327 as for the N ridge to below the couloir, then bear L to foot of the W *kante*. The start of the climb is 3m. L of the *kante* edge and below a dièdre. Climb straight up this dièdre for 20m., then go L to a stance (wedges). Traverse round the *kante* R and up a crack system for 30 m. to an étrier stance. Make a rope traverse L to reach a crack and climb this to a stance on a sloping slab. Traverse below an overhang R for 5m., then turn it. Climb an overhanging chimney and a crack above to a good stance. Now continue up the *kante* for a further 40m. Following this, the ridge eases in steepness and difficulty (9h. from start).

In descent the couloir of Route 327 can be followed without difficulty.

Tower I   2660m.

From North. *Quite an interesting route, but somewhat broken and not sustained. The start is vague and a little difficult to find. III, with a pitch of V. Diagram, p.168.*

330. Soon after the wooden bridge (Route 305) cut across L to foot of the northern rocks. Climb from E to W (L to R) to reach a crack system. Follow this direct to a niche, which is climbed direct; exit direct (V). Now follow the ridge along the crest to top. The descent is best made down a rock gully leading NE (3–4h. from start).

West Edge. *An excellent climb on perfect rock; one of the best on the towers. 200m. V, VI, A1. Seven run-outs. First ascent: Sepp Amrein and Fredy Schwegler, 1 July, 1967. Diagram, p.168.*

331. Follow Route 330 to foot of the tower then work up to below the *kante*. Start the climb 5m. R from the foot, and go up R to a 40m. dièdre. Climb this (17 pegs, 1 wedge) to a stance. Now move L and climb a 20m. crack direct (9 pegs) to below a small roof; étrier stance. Turn the roof R to reach a crack system which is climbed direct for 15m. (11 pegs, 1 wedge) to a dièdre. Follow this for 4m. (3 pegs), leave it R and climb direct (free) to a large roomy stance and crystal hole.

Go straight up for 4m., trend R then return L to the *kante*; stance. Climb the next steep step L (2 pegs) to the first rock teeth of the upper ridge. Go up R to below a white overhang and a stance. Traverse R below the overhang for 10m. (1 peg) then climb direct to a gap in the ridge; stance. Go L from the *kante*, and up a steep section to a dièdre. Follow this for 5m., leave it R and climb the ridge crest to a stance. Now follow the easier block-like ridge to summit. For the descent see Route 330 (10h. for first ascent).

MITTAGSTOCK   2989m.

A large somewhat featureless mtn. due E of the Vorder and Hinter Feldschijen. Compared with these peaks none of the climbing is really good and consequently the mtn. is rarely visited. The best climb would be the W ridge from the Zandlücke (6–7h., III) and the S ridge of the E summit (6–7h. from Zumdorf, III). The normal descent route is the E ridge and SE wall; somewhat unpleasant, being quite difficult and loose. First ascended by Carl Seelig, 14 September, 1901, by the N ridge.

ZAND or ZAHNLÜCKE   2829m.

332. This pass lies between the Mittagstock and the most N-easterly rocks of the Müeterlishorn. It is easily identified by several large impressive granite needles; hence the name.

From the N it is best to follow Route 324 over the Hinter Feldschijenlücke, then bear slightly NE across snow to the lücke (4½–5h.).

  In descent S, go easily over the Rotenbergfirn; old snow and scree; then directly down over the Rinbortalp to Zumdorf (2½–3h.).

SPITZBERG   2934.7m.

The last and most easterly mtn. in the group. There are at least three good climbs, but the NE ridge from the Spitzberglücke (III) is very short (1h.) for the lengthy approach. The S ridge and SE rib are more justifiable in length, especially the latter which is highly recommended. First ascent: R. v Wyss, 30 June, 1901 by the NE ridge with a descent to the Mittaglücke.

South-East Rib. *A very good climb, the best on the Spitzberg.* V, A1.

333. From Zumdorf go over the Rinbortalp to foot of the rib. The climb starts R from a couloir which drops from a pt. just R of the summit. Climb a dièdre then steep rocks to a ledge (V); stance. Now go a few m. R to a 35m. dièdre which is easily seen from below. Climb this (V) and continue up smooth slabs towards an overhanging wall; then climb the next slab to a stance beside a large roof. Go up the L-hand slab to a large terrace and traverse L for a short distance to a wide crack. Climb this to about half height, then continue on the steep slabby edge to a large cracked slab (V, A1, A2); stance. Go L and make awkward step to a block-filled dièdre which is climbed to the ridge (IV). Now follow the ridge pleasantly to summit, climbing over the gendarmes and not avoiding them (8h. from Zumdorf).

South Ridge. *An interesting route but inferior to the SE rib; the main difficulties are constantly avoided.* III. *First ascent: Rudolf Martin and E. W. Weber, 23 July, 1905.*

334. From Blackenstafel, N from Zumdorf, go over scree to a snow couloir in the E flank which leads to the first gap in S ridge. From here make a short traverse E below the very serrated ridge to a smooth groove which is climbed back to the ridge. Now continue below the crest on the W side and finally on the ridge itself to summit (5–6h. from Zumdorf).

Descent of West Ridge to Mittaglücke. I/II. *First ascensionists in descent.*

335. From the summit descend the blocky ridge, avoiding difficulties on S side to the lücke (30 min.). It is also possible to descend N, then down a couloir followed by a traverse across the NW flank to the lücke. This is not quite so easy to follow especially in bad weather.

MITTAGLÜCKE   2765m.

Between the Mittagstock and Spitzberg, but rarely used as a pass. Easy from N but the route is quite difficult to find on the S side in bad weather. This side is seldom ascended so the description given is for the descent. First ascent: E. Labhardt, Alb. Weber and Hugo Schetty, 21 September, 1902.

336. From North. From Gwüest, the small village just below the Göscheneralpsee dam, cut up more or less directly S over steep and tiring terrain to the tiny Mittag glacier which lies between the two northerly arms of the Mittagstock and Spitzberg. Cross snow in the same direction, finally over easy rock and scree to the lücke (4–5h. from Gwüest).

337. Descent to South. There are two ways: (i) Climb directly down to a terrace on the wall below, and follow this W to a distinct rock corner above a steep 50m. rock wall. Go round this corner and climb over slabs to reach a gully which leads down to an easy scree slope (1½h.). Descend this, then down over the Rinbortalp to Zumdorf (2h.).

(ii) From the lücke go about 150m. W towards the Mittagstock, then descend a couloir to snow below (1h.), thence over the Rinbortalp (2h.).

SPITZBERLÜCKE   c.2785m.

The deepest gap in ridge between pt.2852m. and pt.2822m.
The Spitzberg NE ridge (III, 1h.) can be climbed from here
and the serrated W ridge of pt.2804.6m. (III, 1h.) on the
Rossmettlengrat. It serves a useful function as a pass between
Hospental and Göschener Tal.

338. From Gwüest. From the village follow Route 336, but
before the small Mittag glacier bear SE to the NW wall of the
cwm formed by pts.2852m. and 2822m., and climb a steep
narrow gully to the lücke (4–5h.).

On the other side descend scree and easy rocks SE to join
a path leading down to Hospental (2h.).

LOCHSTOCKLÜCKE   c.2650m.

An interesting pass between pts.2696m. and 2570m., W of the
Spitzigrat. It is very useful for the keen walker or mountaineer
who wishes to go from Andermatt to the Göschener Tal,
avoiding the congested road to Göschenen. For the more
experienced the E ridge of the Rossmettlengrat, pt.2804.6m.,
can be climbed (II, 2h.).

339. From North to South. From Abfrutt, just W of Göschenen
at the entrance of the Göschener Tal, take the path SW to
Bortlistafel. Now go up S to the small cwm NW of pts.2696m.
and 2570m., and climb easy rocks to the lücke.

Descend SE, then S past the Rossplattensee (lake). This
upper part is steep and rocky and great care should be taken
in bad weather. Now cut down SE towards Andermatt and
join any of the numerous paths (5–6h., and likewise in the
opposite direction).

INDEX